Better
English
Writing

WEBSTER'S WORD POWER

Better English Writing

GEDDES & GROSSET

WEBSTER'S WORD POWER

Sue Moody, an honours graduate of St Andrews University, has written many learning and teaching materials, and regularly works on a freelance basis for SQA. Sue has written a number of websites for organizations such as the National Library of Scotland, Scottish Natural Heritage and Eneco. Sue has a Diploma with distinction for Freelance and Feature Writing from the London School of Journalism and a Postgraduate Certificate in Primary Education (with distinction) from Moray House. She set up **Bright Writing** in 2004.

This edition published 2015, by Geddes & Grosset,
an imprint of The Gresham Publishing Company Ltd,
Academy Park, Building 4000, Gower Street, Glasgow G51 1PR
www.geddesandgrosset.com
info@geddesandgrosset.co.uk
Find us on facebook/pages/geddesandgrosset

Text by Sue Moody

Copyright © 2014 The Gresham Publishing Company Ltd

ISBN 978-1-84205-759-9

Printed and bound in Spain by Novoprint, S.A.

This book is not published by the original publishers of *Webster's Dictionary* or by their successors.

BETTER ENGLISH WRITING

The aim of this book is to help you write clearer and more concise English – whether you are writing emails or writing a thesis.

By the time you have finished this book, you will have learned tips and techniques to improve your written English and make it more readable and interesting. You will be able to write clearly and effectively, and to come across in a memorable and professional way.

The book contains six main chapters. These are as follows.

Better writing for every day

This chapter gives you some general advice to help you write better English – whatever that type of writing is. It covers the importance of plain English, and will help you to apply the principles of plain English to your writing. We have provided some examples of how not-so-plain English can be converted into plain English!

We also focus on the importance of editing and revising your writing in this chapter. Even the most professional and gifted of writers edit and revise their work.

Writing for learning

In this chapter the focus is on writing for learning. You will find out about research and how to tackle writing essays and theses. There are examples of each of these to give you an idea of what is expected.

You can apply this information to writing assignments for all sorts of courses – whether you are at school, college, university or doing a distance learning course.

Writing for work or business

This chapter gives you the advice and support you need to be able to tackle all sorts of writing for work or business – from writing a CV or making a presentation to get the job, through to communicating with customers by email, letter or text.

There are examples of each type of writing.

Writing for the media

Writing for the media involves learning specific writing techniques. If you are interested in writing articles or news items for newspapers, magazines, ezines, websites, TV or radio, then this chapter will help you to understand and apply these techniques.

It also looks at interview techniques and house styles, and provides useful examples.

Writing creatively

This chapter provides an introduction to the different types of fiction and non-fiction writing, and their characteristics. It also gives you advice on composition techniques that you can apply to your own fiction and non-fiction writing.

Again, examples are provided to illustrate these techniques.

Keep reading and writing!

One of the best ways to improve your own writing is by reading other people's writing. In this chapter, we leave you with some suggestions for material that you should read every day. We also have some suggestions for how you can practise writing regularly – the more you write, the better you'll get.

We hope that you enjoy using this book, and that it will inspire you to produce clear, concise and memorable writing!

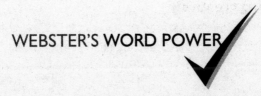

WEBSTER'S **WORD POWER**

CONTENTS

BETTER WRITING FOR EVERY DAY

WRITING FOR LEARNING

WRITING FOR WORK OR BUSINESS

WRITING FOR THE MEDIA

WRITING CREATIVELY

KEEP READING AND WRITING

REFERENCES

BETTER WRITING FOR EVERY DAY

INTRODUCTION

In this chapter, we are going to look at what we mean by plain English and why it is so important. We will then discuss the principles of plain English, and how to apply these to everything you write, whether it's a letter, an email, a marketing brochure or a dissertation.

There are a number of examples to show how not-so-plain English can be transformed into plain English. It really does make a huge difference when you can read and understand something easily the first time round.

Finally, there is a section on the importance of editing and revising your writing, and the role of AutoCorrect, spellcheckers, grammar checkers and Google Translate in this process.

PLAIN ENGLISH

In this section we are going to look at what we mean by 'plain English'.

What is plain English and why is it important?

Plain English writing always keeps the reader in mind, so it is clear and concise and uses the appropriate tone.

Some people think that plain English is oversimplified and that it talks down to readers, as if they were children.

Some people think that writing good English means writing long, convoluted sentences, with lots of clauses, which have, or try to have, impressive, indecipherable words, with regard to making lots of grandiose points in a pompous and grandiloquent way and it would seem not really going anywhere with them at all and, quite frankly, leaving the reader confounded, disconcerted and bewildered, and not understanding at all what the sentence is about because regarding this they go and on and don't seem to know when to stop and in order to get to the end of the sentence the reader has to read the sentence over several times and endeavour hard to understand it, which is quite egregious, don't you agree?

Confused? You should be. This sentence shows why plain English is so important.

Think about why we write in the first place. We write to communicate a message to our reader – not to show how clever or educated or well-read we are. If we can't communicate our message to the reader in a way that they understand then what's the point? We are excluding them, rather than including them.

And apart from anything else, plain English is faster to write and faster to read. People understand your message more easily and respond more positively if it is written using a straightforward and friendly tone, rather than a stuffy and bureaucratic one.

How to apply plain English to your writing

Here are some plain English principles. Apply these to your writing and notice the difference. It can take a while to retrain yourself to write this way, but it's well worth the effort.

Plain English

Think ahead – plan and structure your writing

Ask yourself the following questions before you start to write. If you do this, then you are more likely to produce a well-structured and effective piece of work. If you don't, then your writing is more likely to ramble on, go off at a tangent and not make sense because you don't really know what you want to say.

- What do I want this piece of writing to do?
- What are its aims and outcomes?
- Who are my readers?
- What do I want them to learn/know?
- What do they need/want to learn/know?
- What is the simplest and most effective way of passing on this information?

Make a plan of the structure of your work. How you do this is up to you. Some people think of their piece of writing as a story, and write out main headings and subheadings. Some people make out a list of points, in a logical order. Some people use mind maps. Use a method that you feel comfortable with.

For example, look at the contents page of

this book. The writer used this as a plan for the structure of the book.

Talk directly to your reader – use 'you' and 'we'
Writing doesn't have to be formal and intimidating. You wouldn't **speak** to your reader that way, so you don't need to **write** that way. Try to address your reader personally, and call them 'you' – it will make your writing seem less bureaucratic and intimidating.

Here's an example. If you were applying for a job, which of the following would you prefer to read?

> It is suggested that job applicants submit a handwritten form and hand it in prior to the interview. Applicants will be notified by telephone of their success or otherwise.
>
> or
>
> Please fill in your job application form and hand it in before the interview. We will phone you to let you know if you have been successful.

In the same way, you should also use 'we' or 'I' if you are talking about your business or organisation. It gives a much more direct and positive tone to your writing.

Use simple, straightforward words

People sometimes make the mistake of thinking that by using simple, straightforward words, you are patronising your reader. Quite the opposite – if we're honest, we all prefer to read clear and straightforward text rather than difficult, convoluted text.

There will possibly be times when you have to use technical or more complicated vocabulary because that's what your reader requires, and they will understand the terms and phrases you use. That's fine, as long as your writing remains clear and direct.

In general, always imagine that you are talking to your reader, and stick to straightforward English where possible.

Words and phrases to avoid

Try to avoid using words that most people wouldn't know. For example, you might know what 'egregious' means (outstandingly bad) but it's not a common word, so you're probably safer to use 'shocking' or 'extremely bad' instead.

There are a number of words and phrases that are overused. They don't add anything to your

How to apply plain English to your writing

text, but they do give it a vague and woolly feel. Here are some examples – try to avoid them where possible or use the suggested alternatives.

word/phrase	suggested alternative
as mentioned previously	as we have already said
a number of	some
as regards to/with regards to	about
by means of	by
commence	start
consequently	so
for the purposes of	for
in excess of	more than
in order to	to
in relation to (for example, 'my thoughts in relation to')	on or about (or just leave out)
in the event of	if
inform	tell
necessitate	cause
prior to	before
until such time as	until
utilise	use
whilst	while
with reference to	about

Keep sentences and paragraphs short and concise

Sentences containing lots of clauses (not to mention parentheses – and this is an example) are difficult to read. Many readers give up before they get to the end of long, multi-clause sentences.

Experts on plain English think that an average sentence should be between 15 to 20 words long, although not every sentence has to be the same length. In fact, you can vary them to great effect. Be creative. (Like this!) Try to stick to one idea in each sentence, or at the most one idea and one related point.

It can be quite difficult to keep to short sentences when you are trying to explain something that is complicated. In that case, write your long sentence, then look at ways you can break it up.

The same principles apply to paragraphs. There's nothing more daunting than a long paragraph that deals with so many points that you're lost by the time you reach the end.

Like a sentence, a paragraph is a small, self-contained unit. You state your idea, develop it and then link it to the idea in the next paragraph. If you have planned your writing carefully, your reader will be able to understand each paragraph quickly and easily because they are clear, concise and logical.

Use lists to help you manage information

Sometimes you can't avoid having to cover a lot of information in one section. Lists with bullet points are an excellent way to deal with this. It is easier to take in chunks of information rather than wade through a page full of information that appears to go on and on.

There are two main types of lists.

Here is an example of the first type. It has an introductory statement, followed by a list of separate points. Each point is a complete sentence that begins with a capital letter and ends with a full stop.

Emma wanted to go on a gap year. She had several reasons for this.
She didn't know what she wanted to study at university.
She wanted to travel around the world.
She would never have another chance in her life to take so much time off.

Here is an example of the second type. This list is part of a continuous sentence. Each point starts with a lower case letter, and there is a full stop at the end of the list.

> Emma wanted to go on a gap year because she:
> didn't know what she wanted to study at university
> wanted to travel around the world
> would never have another chance in her life to take so much time off.

Remember that each point in this list has to relate to the introduction. Try reading it to yourself if you're not sure.

For example, does this sound right?

> Emma wanted to go on a gap year because she:
> what she wanted to study at university
> travel around the world
> would never have another chance in her life to take so much time off.

Be active, not passive

An active clause is where **a** *does* something to **b**. In other words, the order is **subject, verb, object**. The verb is active.

For example:

How to apply plain English to your writing

The **candidate completed** the **job application**.

A passive clause is where **b** is done by **a**. In other words, the order is **object, verb, subject**. The verb is passive.

For example:

The job application **was completed** by the candidate.

You'll notice that when you use the passive voice, you have to introduce the words 'was' and 'by', and this can make text more clumsy and long-winded. Passives also de-personalise the text and can sometimes be confusing.

And finally, because you are not talking directly to your reader, you lose your friendly and approachable tone.

Try to use active verbs in the majority of your writing. The passive voice isn't wrong. You need to use it sometimes, but it can be a wordy and unclear way of expressing yourself.

Here are some examples of how to turn passive sentences into active ones:

The land was farmed by student workers. (passive)
Student workers farmed the land. (active)

Plain English

The screenplay was written by a famous author. (passive)
A famous author wrote the screenplay. (active)

The criminals were chased by the police. (passive)
The police chased the criminals. (active)

When passive can be useful
However, there are times when using the passive can be useful.

- It can sound softer:
  The cup has been broken. (passive)
  sounds less accusing than
  You broke the cup. (active)

- You might not know who or what the 'doer' of the sentence is:
  The soldier was awarded a medal for bravery.
  The corner shop has been robbed.

- If it is unclear who or what did something, or if you want to deliberately make it unclear for effect, then you use the passive voice.
  Where are all the sweets that I bought?
  Erm, all those sweets have been eaten. (passive)
  You ate all the sweets, didn't you? (active)

How to apply plain English to your writing

- The passive voice can give an air of objectivity to a text. For example, in a piece of technical text it is not usually acceptable to insert 'I' or 'we' into your conclusions.

  The findings suggest that the vitamin, administered in quantity, does help to prevent the illness. (passive)

  is better than

  We believe that the vitamin, administered in quantity, does help to prevent the illness. (active)

Avoid nominalisation

A nominalisation (how's that for plain English?) is a noun that has been formed from a verb. It is an abstract noun. This means that it is the name of a process, emotion or an idea – something that you can't see, hear, smell or touch. It's not a physical object.

Here are some examples:

verb/adjective	nominalisation
recommend	recommendation
investigate	investigation
discuss	discussion
observe	observation
provide	provision

Nominalisations have the same effect as passive verbs – they can make your writing lack clarity and brevity, and your ideas come across as dull and heavy-going.

Have a look at these examples. In the first sentence, the verb has been nominalised. In the second (**in bold**), it hasn't.

A recommendation regarding shift work was made by senior management.
Senior management recommended shift work.

The implementation of a ban on text speak has been carried out by the school.
The school has implemented a ban on text speak.

She asked for the matter to be put up for discussion.
She asked to discuss the matter.

Tell it like it is!
People can feel uncomfortable about giving commands or instructions (or **imperatives**, as they are called) because they can sound a bit harsh. But then you can take forever to say what you want

and your writing comes across as boring and long-winded. For example:

Customers are advised that they should report to reception on arrival at the building.

You can still use clear and concise commands without sounding like you are barking out an order. Here are some examples:

Customers are advised that they should report to reception on arrival at the building.
Visitors please report to reception.

I would be grateful if you could send the parcel to me.
Please send me the parcel.

The packaging should be removed and the contents of the box should be checked before assembling the furniture.
Remove the packaging and check the contents of the box. Then assemble the furniture.

Examples of plain English and not-so-plain English
The **Plain English Campaign** website has some

Plain English

excellent 'before' and 'after' examples of not-so-plain English. If you can, have a look at this website: www.plainenglish.co.uk

Here are three examples taken from the website showing how to turn not-so-plain English into plain English. Read and enjoy.

Before

High-quality learning environments are a necessary precondition for facilitation and enhancements of the ongoing learning process.

After

Children need good schools if they are to learn properly.

Before

Your enquiry about the use of the entrance area at the library for the purpose of displaying posters and leaflets about Welfare and Supplementary Benefit rights, gives rise to the question of the provenance and authoritativeness of the material to be displayed. Posters and leaflets issued by the Central Office of Information, the Department of Health and Social Security and other authoritative bodies are usually displayed in libraries, but items of a disputatious or polemic kind, whilst not necessarily excluded, are considered individually.

After

Thank you for your letter asking for permission to put up posters in the library. Before we can give you an answer we will need to see a copy of the posters to make sure they won't offend anyone.

Before

Colour: Green

Tax disc: 00000 00000 00000

Expiry: 31/01/2011

Observed from 08:51 to 08:57

A penalty charge of £70 is now payable and must be paid not later than the last day of the period of 28 days beginning with the date on which this PCN was served (i.e. 22/09/2010)

The penalty charge will be reduced by a discount of 50% if it is paid not later than the last day of the period of 14 days beginning with the date on which this PCN was served (i.e. 08/09/2010)

DO NOT PAY THE CIVIL ENFORCEMENT OFFICER

SEE REVERSE FOR:

How to pay

How to appeal to this PCN

What happens if no payment is made

After

Vehicle colour: Green

Number on tax disc: 00000 00000 00000

Date disc expires: 31/01/2111

The traffic warden saw your vehicle was parked illegally from 8:51am to 8:57am.

You must now pay a penalty charge of £70 within 28 days, beginning with the date on which we served this notice (in other words, by 22 September 2010).

We will reduce the penalty charge to £35 if you pay it within 14 days (in other words, by 8 September 2010).

Do not pay the traffic warden.

See the back for:

how to pay;

how to appeal against this notice; and

what happens if you do not pay.

Examples taken from the Plain English website: www.plainenglish.co.uk/examples/before-and-after.html

Why it's essential to revise and edit your writing

REVISING AND EDITING YOUR WRITING

In this section, we are going to focus on why it is important to edit and revise your writing and give you ways to do so.

Why it's essential to revise and edit your writing

No matter what you are writing – whether it's an email or a thesis – it's essential to revise and edit it. There will always be mistakes to correct or things you could improve. Even top writers either edit their own work or use professional editors to do this.

Here is a process for revising and editing your work effectively.

Leave it and go back to it

Once you have finished writing, leave it for a while – even if it's an email and you only leave it for one or two minutes. This will help you to come back to the writing fresh and spot what's right – and what's not.

Have you ever written an angry email and pressed send ... and then regretted it? Giving yourself a bit of time between writing the first

Revising and editing your writing

draft of any piece of text and going back to revise it, can give you a bit more perspective on whether it is good or bad.

Revise the big picture

Read your first draft and concentrate on the big picture, and the overall flow of what you have written. Does it make sense? Is the order logical, or does it need changed?

Does anything need cut or added? What is your overall impression? Ask someone else to read it for you if you're not sure yourself.

Make notes regarding any general observations made about your writing style and bear them in mind the next time you write something.

Edit the detail

Once you are happy with the big picture, you can concentrate on the detail of individual sentences and words. Here are some things to check for:

- Words that have been typed incorrectly (typos) or words that have been misspelled – use a good dictionary to help you check.
- Not-so-plain English – make sure that you have

applied plain English principles and that your writing is clear and concise.
- Misused or confused words.

Here is a short list of some of the most commonly misused or confused words:

accept to agree, to receive or to do
except not including

advice this is the noun, not to be confused with …
advise the verb

complement something that completes or perfects, the number or quantity required to make something complete
compliment an expression of praise, admiration or approval

discreet careful not to attract attention
discrete separate and distinct

ensure make certain that something will happen
insure to provide compensation if a person dies or property is damaged or stolen, etc.

practice this is the noun, not to be confused with …
practise the verb

stationary not moving
stationery writing materials

AutoCorrect, spellcheckers, grammar checkers and Google Translate – use with caution

These features can all be useful if you use them with care, but they can't differentiate between a context that makes sense and one that doesn't. There are pages of hilarious AutoCorrect fails on the internet that show what the problems can be. And Google Translate can often make a literal rather than idiomatic translation. The nature of an idiom is that it may make no sense from the literal meaning of its words but makes more sense in a metaphorical way.

WRITING FOR LEARNING

INTRODUCTION

This chapter will give you guidance on developing the skills you need to write essays and dissertations. Once you have the processes and tools to help you, you can tackle this type of writing more confidently and effectively.

RESEARCH SKILLS

You need to have good research skills to be able to produce essays and theses. Here are some points to help you.

What information are you looking for?
It sounds obvious, but it's worth saying – you need to know what you're looking for before you start looking for it. Make sure you understand the question you are answering, or the task set by your

essay or thesis title. Then you can go on and find the appropriate material to research.

Where can you find that information?

There are many different types and source of information, but the three main ones are books, journals and the internet.

Looking for information can be daunting, so use all the help you can get. When you are looking for **books and journals in the library**, try the following:

- Ask your tutor or teacher for recommendations – which books, journals or periodicals are good for your particular essay or thesis? Is there a reading list for your subject?
- Look through the contents page and index – this will tell you quickly whether the information you are looking for is there.
- Ask the librarian for help if you are having problems using the library cataloguing system.

Where can you find that information?

When you are looking for **information on the internet**, try the following:

- Ask your tutor or teacher for recommendations – which websites are good for your particular essay or thesis?
- Stay focused. Don't go wandering off onto websites that have nothing to do with your project.
- Avoid experiencing information overload by writing a list of questions you want to find answers to, and reject the information that doesn't answer them.
- Stick to two or three sources at one time. You can come back for more.
- Don't go past the first page of your search engine.
- Don't believe everything you read on the internet – stick to reputable sites and those that list traceable sources. If in doubt, check with your tutor or teacher.

Organising your information

Now that you have found your information, don't let it overwhelm you. Organise it and you'll be able to use it effectively:

- Keep going back to the question 'What is it asking?' What information are you looking for?
- Find out how much you are expected to write, so you know when to stop.
- Plan your essay or thesis, so you know what to look for in each section.
- As you are reading, look for the answers to your questions.
- Look for points that agree or disagree with these answers.
- Take notes and summarise the ideas or main points from each piece of information.
- Link these ideas using a mind map, highlighter pens, stickers – whatever you feel comfortable with.
- Ignore any information that is too detailed or not relevant.
- Remember to write down the author, title, place of publication, publisher, date of publication and page numbers for articles from books,

Acknowledging sources/copyright

journals, periodicals and encyclopedias, and web addresses and date of access for online sources. Make sure that web links are current at the time of writing, and convert them to working hyperlinks. This way, you will build a bibliography as you go along – much easier than trying to track down everything you've consulted at the end.

Acknowledging sources/copyright

This last point is very important. You must identify all the material in your essay or thesis that is not your own – no matter where it comes from or what it is. Colleges and universities have strict plagiarism rules which forbid using another person's work without a proper citation. Moreover, if you copy text, diagrams, photographs, art, music or web pages without acknowledging their source, then you are infringing copyright law, and could be prosecuted.

Copyright stays with the originator during his or her lifetime, and with the heirs to their estate for 70 years after their death.

References

Because of the copyright issue, you should make

a list of all the references to books, journals, periodicals and websites you have used in your work. Providing a list of references also provides evidence of how much reading you have done and supports the statements and arguments you make.

You should put references in the main text when you are quoting an author and their work, and also list them separately in a bibliography. Try to avoid using footnotes, unless specified by your institution – they will make your text cluttered.

The **Harvard referencing system** is probably the most common one, although you should check this with your school, college or university – they might use another system instead.

Main text

Here's an example of a **reference or citation** of an author's quote in the main text:

> '[Welsh is] by far the oldest language spoken in Britain today and is among the oldest in Europe ...' (Edwards, 2012, p. 11).

If you quote an author directly like this, you need to show clearly where the quotation begins and ends by using quotation marks. The text in square brackets indicates where you have changed the exact words used by the author in order to suit your sentence (without altering the sense of what was said by the writer). The closing ellipsis indicates that the end of your quote is not the end of the author's statement. If you are quoting the entirety of an author's sentence or statement, this should not be included.

If you aren't quoting the author directly, but want to show that you have read their work, you could write:

> Edwards (2012, p. 11) points out that Welsh is the oldest language spoken in Britain today, as well as being among the oldest in Europe.

Bibliography

Here's how a reference for a **book** would look in the bibliography:

> Edwards, D. I., 2012. *English–Welsh Phrasebook*. Glasgow: Waverley Books, p. 11.

Here's how a reference for a **journal** would look in the bibliography:

Bernard, G. W., 1993. Anne Boleyn's Religion. *The Historical Journal*, 36(01), pp.1–20.

Here's what an **internet reference** would look like in the bibliography:

Bernard, G. W., 1993. Anne Boleyn's Religion. *The Historical Journal*, [online] 36(01). Available from: Cambridge Journals Online
<http://dx.doi.org/10.1017/S0018246X00016083>
[Accessed 29 March 2013].

Beware of cut and paste and plagiarism

Copying and pasting text into your own work without using quotation marks or citing it appropriately is a form of plagiarism.

Plagiarism is when you take somebody else's ideas or writing and present them as your own. If you do this, you will probably fail your essay or thesis, if not face disciplinary action.

When you are taking notes, decide what information you need from your source, and then write or summarise it in your own words. That way, you won't be tempted – consciously or subconsciously – to copy the source, word for word.

The process of writing an essay

Don't cut and paste. You can easily forget that you have taken somebody else's work and put it into your own – especially if you change the font to the one you are using.

Remember that plagiarism is cheating.

ESSAYS

Whether you are at school, college, university or any other type of learning institution, you will have to write essays at some point in your course. It's one of the most common ways of assessing learners.

In this section, we will help you to use your research to plan and write clear, concise and high quality essays.

The process of writing an essay

There is a process involved in writing an essay. This process doesn't have to be linear, where each stage is only done once. You can repeat different parts of the process and revise your work until you are happy with it.

Here's an example of a process you could use:

- **Analyse the question or title of your essay**. What is it asking for? How are you going to answer it? Many teachers and tutors say that this is where many students fall down – they don't stay relevant to their theme because they don't keep looking back at what the question is asking for.

- **Brainstorm your ideas.** People often find it very stressful when they are faced with writing an essay because they don't know where to start. Don't panic. Instead, get some paper and write down all your ideas about the title, what your structure might be and where you might look for evidence. If it helps, do this with a friend or colleague. Don't try to sort anything out at this stage. That can come later.

- **Research. Read around the question/title and make relevant notes.** Don't waste time on irrelevant reading or too much detail. Keep the length of the essay in mind. Focus. Take notes (in your own words) and keep full reference details (including page numbers of direct quotes) of all the material you have looked at and think you will use.

Planning your essay

- **Plan your structure**. You need to do this to help you answer the question and develop a clear argument, so keep referring back to the question to make sure that your structure is relevant.
- **Write the first draft.** Remember to write in plain English.
- **Include full references and a bibliography**.
- **Revise and edit your work.** Refer back to Chapter 2 (*see* page 47) if you're not sure where to start.
- **Identify any missing information.** Editing usually reveals where there are gaps in your writing.
- **Cut out anything you don't need.** Editing also reveals repetition and unnecessary detail.
- **Write the final draft.**

Planning your essay

You need to plan your essay. This will help you to organise your thoughts, and will stop you from wandering off the point, getting lost and writing lots of irrelevant and unnecessary words.

Planning will help you to write a powerful introduction, develop your argument and summarise its main points effectively and concisely in the conclusion.

Imagine that you have been given the following essay title from your history tutor:

Account for the failure of American policy in Vietnam from 1956–73.

You have analysed the title, brainstormed your ideas and carried out your research. Now it's time to plan your essay. Here's one example of how you can do this.

You'll probably have gathered a lot of information, so drawing a mind map can help you to empty your head of that information, and organise it into logical chunks.

- Get a piece of paper and write down all your ideas – don't worry about perfect writing at this point – just get the content down.
- Get a clean piece of paper. Put the topic box in the middle of the page.
- Now think about the main ideas of your report – what are they?
- Draw lines from the topic box to these main ideas.

Structuring your essay

- Now add information where you think it sits within these main ideas.
- Make links between the main ideas.

Structuring your essay

Giving your essay a structure like the one below will help you to answer the question and create a tight and consistent argument:

- Introduction
- Development
- Conclusion

Here's an example of how we could use this structure for our essay title above.

Introduction

- This essay is going to account for the failure of American policy in Vietnam.
- America strong and powerful – so why did it go wrong? Reasons: ineffective military approach; poor morale; media coverage; atrocities; cost in lives and material resources; communism no longer a threat in 1973.
- Essay to analyse each of these factors in turn to account for failure of American policy.

Essays

- First, need to analyse why America joined the war.

Development

Background to war – why USA joined in first place.

- 'Domino effect' – spread of communism in south-east Asia.
- North Vietnam communist.
- USA supported South Vietnam to prevent spread of communism.

Military tactics – failure

- US troops inexperienced.
- Mainly young white working-class or black boys (many white middle-class boys escaped to college or Canada).
- Troops didn't want to be there and didn't understand why they were there – 8000 miles from home fighting for what? Therefore low morale, drug taking, killing officers, deserting.
- Compare to the Vietcong – hardened, experienced guerrilla fighters – who had been fighting for independence since Japanese left at end of the Second World War. Desperate to kick Americans out of their country at any cost.
- US high-tech military tactics didn't work against Vietcong guerrilla warfare.

Structuring your essay

- US tactics alienated South Vietnamese, and they helped Vietcong in some cases.

Media coverage

- A TV in most American living rooms – coverage of the war reached most Americans.
- Public witnessed the horror of the war and US failures.
- Resulted in propaganda, including protest songs.
- Martin Luther King preached against war.
- All this swung public opinion against war.

This was not helped by:

US atrocities

- For example, massacre at My Lai of hundreds of unarmed civilians in South Vietnam.
- Other war crimes reported to public at home.
- This caused outrage and undermined the moral authority of USA to continue war.

Cost in terms of material and human resources

- Tens of thousands of American troops killed and hundreds of thousands of troops wounded.
- Huge numbers of Vietnamese killed.
- President Johnson had to cancel his Great Society

Essays

programme – huge financial cost to USA that wasn't sustainable.

Better relationships between America, Russia and China

- Cold war starting to thaw.
- Communism not such a threat.
- What was the point?

Conclusion

- Summarise these factors succinctly and concisely – end with quote 'For the American public, Vietnam had been a terrible lesson on the limits of their power – why, exactly, had these young men been sent to their deaths? No one seemed able to answer this question.' (Quote from *National Qualifications Curriculum Support: The origins and development of the Cold War, 1945–85* (Learning and Teaching Scotland, 2008).

Writing the introduction

The introduction should:

- set the question or title in its wider context

Writing the introduction

by giving background information about the
central issue
• explain the main ideas of your argument and
how you are going to answer the question
• make a link to the first point in the 'Development'
section.

Here's an example of an introduction that
covers these points.

Account for the failure of American policy in Vietnam from 1956–73

America entered the war in Vietnam to stop the spread of
communism, promote democracy and support its allies. It
had access to great power and resources and the latest
military technology, so what went wrong, and why did it
pull out of Vietnam in 1973?

There are a number of factors that account for
the failure of American policy in Vietnam from 1956–
73. First, America's high-tech military approach was
not appropriate for dealing with the guerrilla tactics
used by the Vietcong, and its troops were young and
inexperienced, and didn't understand what or why they
were fighting. The Vietcong, on the other hand, were

Essays

experienced, war-hardened and determined to drive the Americans out.

Second, extensive media coverage brought the full horror and failures of the war into people's living rooms like never before, and turned American public opinion against it.

Third, atrocities such as the massacre at My Lai undermined the moral authority of the US to continue the war.

Fourth, the cost of the war in terms of material and human resources was huge.

Finally, the political background had changed during the years 1956–73, and by the time Nixon came to power relations between America, Russia and China were much friendlier. Communism wasn't the threat it had been in the 1950s and 1960s, so by 1973 most Americans didn't understand the point of the war.

This essay will analyse each of these factors in turn.

But to account for the failure of American policy in Vietnam, we first have to analyse why America joined the war in the first place.

Developing the argument

The middle part of your essay must develop the arguments you set out in your introduction, and it must support your final conclusions.

Developing the argument

This is where a good structure is really useful. This will help you to stay relevant to your theme while you expand on and explain your ideas and provide relevant references and examples to support them.

You should write clearly and concisely. You can still write in plain English, although an academic style is more likely to use the third person (he, she or it) instead of the second person (you and we), and some institutions may insist upon third person.

For example:

> America entered the war in Vietnam in the winter of 1955. Its goals were to stop the spread of communism, encourage democracy and support its allies.

Remember to write critically, not descriptively. One of the biggest criticisms that teachers and tutors have of their students is that they just regurgitate the facts, rather than analysing and evaluating those facts. Don't just say that something happened – say why or how it happened and back it up with evidence.

For example:

Essays

America's intervention was set against an increasing concern about the spread of communism in south-east Asia. The Americans were convinced that they should actively support countries like South Vietnam, Laos, Cambodia, Thailand and Burma to prevent this from happening. As President Eisenhower said at a press conference on 7 April 1954, 'You have a row of dominoes set up. You knock over the first one, and what will happen to the last one is a certainty, that it will go over very quickly.'

Make sure that you link each idea or point to the next one, so that your argument flows logically and smoothly.

Writing the conclusion

The conclusion should:

- recap on and answer the essay title
- summarise and evaluate the main arguments
- highlight the most important aspect or aspects covered.

Here's an example:

To conclude, American policy in Vietnam failed because of ineffective military tactics; the strength of public opinion

Writing the conclusion

due to negative media coverage of US failures and atrocities; the huge cost in terms of money and human life and the emergence of détente between America, Russia and China. Military tactics failed because no matter how advanced the American technology, they could not beat the guerrilla tactics or motivation of the Vietcong, who were on home terrain and had years of fighting experience. Compare this to the American troops, who were young and inexperienced, and did not want to fight in a war they did not understand. To begin with, the American public backed what they saw as a war against communism, but media exposure of the US failures and atrocities and protest by public figures and popular musicians swung public opinion the other way. The sheer cost in terms of life and money was not sustainable in the long term. But perhaps the most compelling reason for failure was that by 1973, the reason for the war no longer existed because of the easing relations between America, China and the USSR. This was a particularly humiliating failure because 'For the American public, Vietnam had been a terrible lesson on the limits of their power – why, exactly, had these young men been sent to their deaths? No one seemed able to answer this question.'

(*The origins and development of the Cold War*, 1945–85 [2008])

THESES/DISSERTATIONS

If you have completed postgraduate research, or are completing your Master's, PhD or doctorate, then you will have to write a thesis or a dissertation. This will be the culmination of in-depth study in your chosen subject or discipline. You will probably already have gathered a lot of research data and will have been writing as you go – so you're not starting with a blank sheet of paper.

Some people find the thought of writing a thesis quite daunting. It's a good idea to review other theses in your research area, to see how these have been tackled.

This section will help you to plan, structure and write a high quality thesis.

The following principles are the same for writing essays as they are for writing a thesis:

- planning and structuring your work
- creating a powerful introduction
- developing the argument
- linking ideas from one section to the next
- writing strong and authoritative conclusions.

The process of writing a thesis

It is therefore worth revisiting the examples in the 'Essay' section before you read this section.

The process of writing a thesis

As with essay writing, think of writing your thesis as a process to go through. This should help to give you focus if you are feeling stressed and don't know where to start.

- Think about a **general structure** for your thesis as soon as you can. It will help you to focus your research and write material that is relevant to your topic/argument.

- **Write as you go along.** This is an important part of the research process because it makes you think about what you are doing, analyse information and make connections. It also means that you will be tackling your thesis in small chunks, rather than doing it all at once at the end.

- Remember while you are doing this to **record all your references**. It's much easier to do this just now, rather than try to go back and locate sources at the end.

- **Develop a filing system**. This should reflect

the general structure of your thesis and could be organised around different chapters or research data.

Each time you produce writing or notes on a particular aspect of your thesis, put it in here. Use envelopes, plastic folders, paper folders – anything that works for you. That way you have the beginnings of your thesis, ready to work on.

- **Report back to your supervisor** regularly and show them your writing. Ask for feedback. Better to do this gradually rather than in one huge chunk at the end.

- **Write a first draft**. Remember to apply the rules of plain English. Go back to Chapter 2 to remind yourself of these.

- **Revise and edit your thesis**. Check your word limit, and keep this in mind while you are doing this. You'll probably have to go through this loop a few times before you are finished. Go back to chapter 2 to remind yourself of techniques for revising and editing your work.

- **Published thesis.** Congratulations!

Planning your thesis

Planning your thesis is essential if you want to:

Planning your thesis

- create a logical, consistent argument
- stay relevant to your theme
- make it concise and easy for the reader to understand.

We've already looked at using a mind map to help you plan your writing (*see* section on 'Essays', page 62).

You could also try the following method:

- Brainstorm all the ideas and information that you need to include in your thesis on a large sheet of paper – include ideas for chapter headings and how you are going to analyse and represent your research. Don't bother about perfect writing – just get everything down.
- Start to sort this into chapter headings and sub-headings. For example, you might have used a number of different methods to conduct your research, so each method will need its own sub-heading. You could have another sub-heading at the end of the chapter to bring together all these methods.
- Add notes, references and conclusions as you go.

You have now built up a plan that will help you to see where you have gaps in your research and also where you have irrelevant information that you can drop.

Remember to get regular feedback from your supervisor – this will also help the planning process.

Now you are ready to use this plan to help you create a more detailed structure.

Structuring your thesis

Here is an example of a suggested structure, although your institution might have variations on this. You are best to check with your supervisor before you begin.

- Title page
- Abstract
- Acknowledgements
- Contents page
- Introduction
- Literature review
- Materials and methods
- Results/Findings
- Discussion

Sections within the structure

- Conclusions
- References
- Appendices

Sections within the structure

Let's look at what each of these sections involves in more detail. Ask your supervisor to give you examples of published theses in your research area to find out how other people have tackled these sections.

Title page

This tells your reader straightaway what your thesis is about. Make it concise, and clear. It must describe to your reader quickly and effectively what your research is about. Your institution will probably have a standard format that you have to follow, so check this with your supervisor.

Abstract

An abstract is the summary of your research. It needs to summarise clearly and succinctly what you did and why you did it, and it needs to be able to stand alone – if your thesis is registered within a database, it becomes a document in its own right.

You should probably write your abstract last, when the whole thesis is fresh in your mind. Remember that it usually has a word limit, and is often only one page long. Plain English is essential here.

Acknowledgements
This is where you acknowledge people who have helped and advised you.

Contents page (can also include lists of tables, illustrations and figures)
This is basically the structure of your thesis, and should show how balanced (or not!) the sections are.

Introduction
The introduction should give the reader more detail about the research summarised in the abstract and flag up the content in the thesis.

The literature review
This chapter shows where your particular piece of research fits into the overall context of your research field. What does your thesis add to this area of research? You need to identify this and

Sections within the structure

state the research question or problem you will be addressing in your thesis.

Materials and methods

This is a clear and concise description of how you conducted your research. For example, you could have used particular equipment, processes or materials. It's a fine balance here – you need to give enough detail for another researcher to understand what you have done.

Results/Findings

Ask your supervisor about this. Science theses usually have separate sections for the results and the discussion of the results. A psychology thesis, however, might combine both in one chapter called *findings*.

Discussion

This section is where you review your own research in the context of your chosen field and discuss what it has added.

Conclusions

This section should summarise your research,

describe the main points that have emerged and suggest what they mean for your chosen field.

References

Keeping note of your references as you go along is even more important when you are writing a thesis. When you are going through the revision and editing process, you will probably add and take away some references, so before you submit your thesis, check that all the references in your reference list are actually in the text, and all the references in the text are in the reference list.

Your supervisor will tell you which referencing style to use.

Appendices

Appendices usually contain information that is important to your research, but which takes up too much space or doesn't sit happily in the main body of the text.

Good luck if you are writing a thesis. This will probably be the most challenging thing that you do in your academic career. Follow these tips, work

Sections within the structure

with your supervisor and you will be the proud owner of a bound copy of the culmination of your work that other people will use in their research.

WRITING FOR WORK OR BUSINESS

INTRODUCTION

Whether you are an employee or running your own business, you must be able to put your ideas across as clearly and concisely as possible in a variety of different situations.

This section will ensure that you come across in a memorable and professional way. It will give you guidance on the following aspects of business writing:

- how to apply for a job
- emails and texting in the office
- emails and letters to customers
- reports
- presentations
- marketing and promotional writing
- writing announcements.

APPLYING FOR A JOB

This section focuses on improving your writing skills to help you apply for a job. It also gives advice on how to write a reference for somebody who is applying for a job.

How to write an effective CV

A CV, or curriculum vitae, is a brief description of your personal details, education and work history. Most employers will ask for your CV as part of your job application. It needs to be concise, clear, organised and well presented, because you will probably be competing with lots of other people. A good CV is more likely to get you an interview.

In this section, we'll go over how to create your own CV and show you an example of a finished CV.

Personal details
You need to provide your:

- name
- address
- day and evening telephone numbers
- email
- age.

How to write an effective CV

Be honest about this information – if an employer discovers you've been lying, you definitely won't get the job.

Education and qualifications

This is where you give details of your education and any qualifications you have. Put these in reverse chronological order – most recent first, and oldest last.

Work experience

List all the jobs you have had in this section. Again, put this information in reverse chronological order (most recent first). You need to provide:

- the starting and finishing date for each job
- your work title
- who you worked for
- where you worked and a description of what you did.
- Keep sentences short, concise and relevant.

Further information

In this section, put down any other skills, qualifications or information that you think will make a good impression and help you to get the job. For example, if you have a clean driving licence, and this is relevant to the job, then include this information.

Interests

This is where you can describe what your interests or hobbies are. You can also use it to give a glimpse of your personality, but try to bear in mind whether mentioning it will put you in a positive or negative light. Again, you need to be honest here, but not too honest.

For example, if you are a computer games addict, and do nothing much else in your spare time, you could express this in a more positive way by saying: "I have an encyclopedic knowledge of gaming and video games." Sounds a bit geeky but, then again, geeks are usually intelligent. You might love parties – instead call it 'entertaining at home' but don't go into too many details.

Some outside interests might not appear to be immediately relevant to the job but show you to be friendly, sociable, good at organising etc. Clubs, societies, choirs and sports clubs, especially those in which you have a role, all show positive characterstics that will be useful in any job.

How to write an effective CV

Referees

Choose two people who can provide references for you. One should provide a personal reference (usually somebody you have known for a long time) and one a professional reference (usually somebody you have worked for).

Your referees must not be related to you. Remember to ask their permission and check their details before you include them.

Example of a CV

Curriculum Vitae
Personal details

Anne Other

The Cottage

Elm Street

Goldenvalley

GO13 7AN

telephone: 01337 888 888

mobile: 07777 999999

email: anne.other@wordsolutions.co.uk

date of birth: 07/04/60

Applying for a job

Education and qualifications

National School of Journalism (2010–2012)
Freelance and Feature Writing Course (distinction)
Goldenvalley College of Education (1987–88)
Postgraduate Certificate in Primary Education
(distinction)
*Newtown College of Commerce and Technology
(1982–83)*
Diploma for Graduate Secretaries
Cowper University (1978–82)
MA Hons in Medieval History (2:1)

Work experience

June 2011 – present

Director: Word Solutions Ltd, Goldenvalley
Word Solutions (formerly Publishing Solutions Ltd) offers
professional writing and research services.

January 2004 – June 2011

Director: Publishing Solutions Ltd, Goldenvalley
Publishing Solutions offered the following services:

- researching and writing original material
- carrying out in-field research and writing evaluations
- rewriting existing material
- editing and proofreading
- project management.

How to write an effective CV

September 1992 – December 2003

Head of Publishing: Goldenvalley Education Council, Goldenvalley

I had responsibility for:

- acting as editor-in-chief
- building up a list of freelance designers, editors and proofreaders
- publishing curriculum material
- writing and publishing corporate literature.

May 1991 – August 1992

Professional Officer: Goldenvalley Education Council, Goldenvalley

I had responsibility for:

- helping with curriculum initiatives
- researching, writing and publishing education material
- initiating promotional material.

September 1988 – April 1991

Primary Education Officer: Goldenvalley Design Council, Goldenvalley

I had responsibility for:

- researching and writing copy for the design newsletter

Applying for a job

- providing inservice on design and technology for primary schools in Goldenvalley
- writing and publishing inservice material
- liaising with sponsor bodies to write and publish case study materials on design and technology.

Further information

I am a member of the Society for Editors and Proofreaders.

I hold a clean driving licence.

Interests

Music is a passion. I play the violin in an amateur orchestra and go to concerts regularly.

I am interested in all aspects of the arts.

I am an avid reader.

Referees

Referee 1

Title
address
telephone number
email address

Referee 2

Title
address
telephone number
email address

How to write an effective covering letter

Role of the covering letter

A covering letter builds on the information you provide in your CV. It is your chance to say why the company should employ you. This letter should tell the reader that you are the right person for the job.

Do your research before you write

Before you write your letter, do some research on the company and the job for which you are applying. If you do this, you will show that you have used your initiative and that you are genuinely interested in the job. Research will also help you to find out whether the company is formal or relaxed, new or established. You can then pitch your letter using the appropriate style of language and terminology.

Format

Put your address at the top right hand corner of the letter. Miss a line and then put the date. The address of the person you are writing to goes on the left hand side after the date.

Applying for a job

Date

This is usually written as 10 July 2012 rather than 10th July 2012.

Address

Put in the person's name, title, address and post-code. You don't need commas after each line in the address, or full stops after people's initials.

Greeting

- If you are on first name terms with the person, use 'Dear Anne'.
- If not, then use 'Dear Mr Other' or 'Miss Other/ Mrs Other'.
- If you are writing to a woman and don't know what her title is, then use 'Ms'.
- If you don't know the person's name, then use 'Dear Sir' or 'Dear Madam'.
- If you don't know whether they are male or female, use 'Dear Sir or Madam'.
- You don't need a comma after the greeting.

Headings

If you feel a heading would be useful, then put it in bold and upper and lower case.

Don't use 're:'.

How to write an effective covering letter

Main body of the letter

Make sure you are writing in plain English and keep your writing clear and concise. Use bold type to emphasise any points – lots of capitals or italics are hard to read.

The opening paragraph should be short, sharp and effective.

The second paragraph should describe the professional and academic qualifications that you have that are relevant to the job.

The third paragraph should emphasise what you can do for the company. You should expand on the relevant points in your CV.

The fourth paragraph is where you can say that you would welcome an interview.

Ending

If you used the first name of the person in the greeting, then sign off with 'Yours sincerely'.

If you used the formal title of the person in the greeting, then sign off with 'Yours faithfully'.

If you know the person well, then you can sign off with whatever you think is most appropriate – for example, 'Best wishes' or 'Yours truly'.

You don't need a comma after the ending.

Applying for a job

Enclosures

If you have attached any material, put 'Enc' or 'Encs' at the end of your letter. This stands for 'enclosure' or 'enclosures'.

Check the letter over before you send it off.

Example of a covering letter for a job application

Anne Other

The Cottage

Elm Street

Goldenvalley

GO13 7AN

10 July 2011

James Brown

Head of Education

Goldenvalley Architecture and Design

Market Street

Goldenvalley

GO11 6BQ

Dear Mr Brown

I am writing to apply for the post of writer for goldenvalleyarchitecture.com magazine, which was

How to write an effective covering letter

advertised on the Architecture and Design News website.

I have an Honours degree in Medieval History. This has enabled me to develop skills in researching, synthesising and analysing information, and to write clearly and concisely. In addition, I have a diploma with distinction from the National School of Journalism, and understand the styles and techniques required for magazine writing.

I believe that professional writers should be able to apply their skills to any subject. For example, I have been asked to research and write about subjects as diverse as Watt's steam engine and sustainable development education in Sweden. However, I do thoroughly understand the general principles of design, and the importance of the design brief, because I worked for the Goldenvalley Design Council for two years.

I have enclosed a portfolio of some of my work. I hope that this convinces you that I have the experience, skills and enthusiasm to write high quality copy for your web magazine.

I would be happy to bring examples of my work to an interview. My contact details are on my CV.

Yours faithfully

Anne Other

Encs

How to write a reference

You might be asked to write a reference for somebody who is applying for a job.

A reference letter should provide information on who you are, your position, your connection with the person you are recommending, why they are qualified for the job, and the specific skills they have. You should also provide contact information for any follow-up.

Refer back to the 'How to write a covering letter' section (*see* page 91) to remind yourself of how to lay out your address, date, reader's address and ending.

Greeting

If a named person has requested the reference, then use 'Dear Mr', 'Dear Miss', 'Dear Mrs' or 'Dear Ms' depending on what is appropriate.

If you are writing a general letter, then use 'To whom it may concern' or leave the greeting out altogether.

Main body of the letter

The first paragraph should explain your connection

How to write a reference

to the person you are recommending. How do you know them, and why are you qualified to write a reference for them?

The second paragraph should contain specific information about the person you are recommending. What qualifications and skills do they have that will contribute to the job? You might have to split this information into several paragraphs.

The third paragraph should relate the candidate's qualifications, skills and experience directly to the post. Look at the job description to help you do this.

Summarise why the candidate is suitable for the job, and why you are recommending them. You can state that you 'highly recommend' or 'thoroughly recommend' the person, or something else along those lines.

Conclusion

Offer to provide the reader with more information, and provide your contact details (phone numbers and email address).

Applying for a job

Example of a reference

Anne Other
The Cottage
Elm Street
Goldenvalley
GO13 7AN
10 July 2011

Ms Jane Nother
HR Department
Cowper University
Aberford
AD16 7NN

Dear Ms Nother

Sandra Wilson worked for me as Publications Assistant from 1993 to 2003 while I was Head of Publishing at AAA Publishing Ltd.

Sandra was a valuable asset to the publications team. She helped me to set up the processes and systems necessary for a very busy publishing department, and provided excellent administrative support. Sandra had to work under considerable stress and I relied upon her heavily.

How to write a reference

Sandra has studied an HNC in Business Administration and a Diploma in Management. She has also taken courses to improve her skills in Microsoft Excel, Word and Project.

Sandra is a self-improver, and is always willing to learn new things. She would be able to fit in immediately to the role of Secretary, because she has the necessary skills and qualifications. Sandra has all the skills that you are looking for. She:

- is an extremely organised, reliable and efficient person, and can manage her own workload without supervision
- can answer the phone and deal with enquiries effectively and diplomatically
- keeps a cool head under stress – Sandra's patience was tested many times while I was Head of Publishing, but she always remained calm and diplomatic
- can keep a diary and timetable appointments effectively – she not only did this for me, but also set up a very successful and efficient spreadsheet for the department
- can deal with correspondence efficiently and effectively because of her knowledge of the Microsoft Office suite of software

Applying for a job

- can be trusted with confidential information – she is discreet and loyal.

I would thoroughly recommend Sandra for this post. Her efficiency, organisational and administrative skills, reliability and initiative make her an ideal candidate.

Please do not hesitate to contact me if you need any further information.

Yours faithfully

Anne Other
Director, Word Solutions
anne.other@wordsolutions.co.uk
01337 888 999
07777 999999

Presentations

If your CV and covering letter are successful, you'll be invited for an interview. This can sometimes involve making a presentation to an interview panel. Lots of people shake in their boots at the thought of this, but if you prepare a simple, clear and concise presentation, then it will be an excellent prop and a tool for helping you to get the job. We have covered presentations later on in this chapter.

EMAILS AND TEXTING IN THE WORKPLACE

This section gives you guidance on emailing and texting at work.

General approach

Emailing and texting are now the most common ways of communicating at work. Because people tend to use more informal language when communicating in these ways than they do when they are writing a business letter, however, some people think that it is acceptable to relax the rules of grammar, punctuation and clear writing. This is not the case. No matter what you are writing, it needs to be clear and easy to understand, or you won't get your message across. This applies to emailing and texting at work.

Here are some points to keep in mind when you are emailing:

- Be clear and concise. If you have a lot of information, send it as an attachment.
- Put the title of the email in the subject box, and keep it short.
- Keep paragraphs short and use bulleted lists.

Emails and texting in the workplace

There's nothing worse than scrolling through screeds of information.

- Don't overuse capitals. They can look aggressive and 'shouty'.
- Don't attach pictures or documents that are over 5MB. This can cause problems for the person on the receiving end.
- Reply to an email as soon as possible, but don't keep replying unnecessarily ('thanks!', 'it's a pleasure!', 'no problem!'). It takes up valuable time, you will get into a never-ending cycle and it will clog up your inbox.

Style and tone

When you are emailing or texting colleagues, you should remember that you are at work, and that they are colleagues, and not friends. While it's acceptable to use a more relaxed tone, here are some points to keep in mind:

- Don't use slang, abbreviations or emoticons. It's not professional.
- Remember also to use proper grammar and formatting. If you use lower case and ignore

proper sentence structure, you will come across as sloppy and unprofessional.

- Think about your reader and the most appropriate way to open and close your email. If you are emailing your boss, it might be more appropriate to open with 'Dear Ms Other' and close with 'Regards' than to open with 'Hi' and close with 'Cheers'. If you are emailing a colleague who is also a friend, then 'Hi' and 'Cheers' are acceptable.

Text-speak?

What is text-speak? The term describes the dialect sometimes used in digital communication whereby lengthy sentences and thoughts are condensed down, using phonetic abbreviations and substituted letters, numbers and characters.

Here's an example. See if you can translate:

My hols this yr wr CWOT. I wnted 2go2 NY but my bro didn't. We wnt to Florida instd but it ws full of :-@ kids in theme pks n I h8d it.

Here's the translation:

My holidays this year were a complete waste of time. I

Emails and texting in the workplace

wanted to go to New York, but my brother didn't. We went to Florida instead, but it was full of screaming kids in theme parks and I hated it.

How long did it take you to work that out? It's certainly nothing like as clear as plain English and it's just not appropriate in a work environment. Apart from coming over as unprofessional, you are much more likely to be misunderstood.

Even for those who would not use this kind of extreme text-speak, we often write in a markedly different way when texting or emailing than we would on the page, without, for example, paying the same attention to grammar and punctuation.

While this is fine for personal communication, it carries the same problems, if to a lesser degree, that text-speak does when it comes to work correspondence. Meanings can easily become ambiguous and unclear to the recipient, and, even if clear enough, your message still comes across as sloppy and unprofessional. Stick to plain English when you are emailing and texting at work.

Good practice

Good practice

Here's an example of an email exchange between colleagues. It is informal and friendly, but still remains professional:

From: john.smith@wordsolutions.co.uk
To: anne.other@wordsolutions.co.uk
Cc: george.brown@wordsolutions.co.uk
Subject: Notes for board meeting

Hi Anne

Could you please bring last month's notes along with you to the Board meeting today. This should help to focus our discussions and hopefully we'll finish in time for a cup of coffee.

Thanks for your help with editing the minutes, by the way.

Best wishes,
John

Emails and texting in the workplace

From: anne.other@wordsolutions.co.uk
To: john.smith@wordsolutions.co.uk
Cc: george.brown@wordsolutions.co.uk
Subject: Re: Notes for board meeting

Hello John

No problem at all. I'll bring the notes in before the meeting.

Yes, here's hoping that we get through it all quickly!

Delighted to help with the editing.

Best regards,
Anne

EMALS AND LETTERS

This section focuses on writing emails and letters in the workplace. This time we're focussing on writing to customers.

General approach

When you are emailing and writing letters to customers, it's even more important to take the right approach. Informal and sloppy messages are unprofessional and just won't do. Imagine you are a customer and receive a letter in text-speak in response to a complaint. How would you feel? You would probably think that you weren't being taken seriously, or that your complaint wasn't being dealt with in a professional way. We've said it before and we'll say it again – no matter what you are writing, it needs to be clear and easy to understand, or you won't get your message across. This is essential when you are communicating with customers.

Keep the following points in mind when you are emailing or writing to customers:

- Be clear and concise.
- If you are writing a letter and it has a lot of

information, break it up into short paragraphs with subheadings.

- If you are writing an email, send any large chunks of additional information as an attachment.
- Always remember that you are writing to a customer and be professional in your approach.

Style and tone

When you are writing emails or letters to customers, your style and tone should be formal and professional. Don't use slang, abbreviations, emoticons or text-speak:

> Soz I 4got 2 send the order, bro

It's difficult to understand, unprofessional and will therefore give a bad impression of both you and your organisation.

Remember also to use proper grammar, spelling, punctuation and formatting. If you use lower case where there should be a capital letter and ignore proper sentence structure, you will come across as sloppy and unprofessional.

Here's an example:

> their wasn't any things left in wearhouse sorry I didn't get the order by you.

House style

A house style is a set of rules that states how all documents and written communications from a business should be formatted.

The aim of house style is to present a recognisable, consistent image of a company to the outside world. Your company will probably have a house style, so check this out before you start to write emails or letters.

House style covers things like:

- font style and size – for example, don't use Times Roman if the house style uses Arial
- colours used – for example, house style might use dark blue text in emails and letters, rather than black
- whether text should be right justified, left justified, centred or unjustified
- how the address and contact details should be presented.

Good practice

The section on 'Emails and texting in the office' will remind you of the basics of writing a business email. 'How to write an effective covering letter' in the 'Applying for a job' section in this chapter will remind you of the basic format and structure of a business letter. Here are some key points about writing emails and letters specifically for customers, followed by an example of an email and a letter to a customer.

Writing emails to customers

Here are some key points:

- Don't use 'Hi'. Use 'Dear Mr, Miss, Mrs or Ms'.
- Take as much time and care with an email as you would do with a letter.
- Use 'plain text' rather than HTML (this creates emails that are in the style of web pages). Some people will be accessing their emails from hand-held devices such as smartphones that can only display text.
- Structure your email as you would a letter – that is, with a beginning, middle and end. This will help the reader to understand what you are writing quickly and easily.
- Break up long paragraphs and use bulleted lists. This helps the reader to digest large chunks of information.

Good practice

- Don't attach files or images that are bigger than 5MB because this can cause problems for the person receiving your email.
- Remember that your company's disclaimer probably won't protect you if you deliberately mislead your customer or lie to them.

Always check over an email before you send it out.

Example of an email to a customer

From:	julie.brown@glassesforyou.com
Sent:	21 January 2013 12.07
To:	johnsmith@brownandbrown.com
Subject:	Delivery of broken crystal glasses

Dear Mr Smith

Thank you for your email of 21 July 2012, informing us that three of the six crystal glasses you ordered from our website were broken on arrival.

We are extremely sorry about this. We have systems and procedures in place to make sure that our fragile glassware is packed as carefully as possible, and are looking into why these failed in your case. We will email you when we have found out what happened.

You told us in your email that these glasses are needed urgently for a wedding present, so we have packed another box and will send it by courier to your work address in Edinburgh today. It will arrive by 4.30pm at the latest.

We hope that this will make up for your earlier disappointment, and look forward to have you shopping with us again in the future.

Yours sincerely
Julie Brown
Customer Services Manager
julie.brown@glassesforyou.com
www.glassesforyou.com
0171 888 888

From:	julie.brown@glassesforyou.com
Sent:	21 January 2013 12.07
To:	johnsmith@brownandbrown.com
Subject:	Delivery of broken crystal glasses

Dear Mr Smith

Thank you for your email of 21 July 2012, informing us that three of the six crystal glasses you ordered from our website were broken on arrival.

We are extremely sorry about this. We have systems and procedures in place to make sure that our fragile glassware is packed as carefully as possible, and are looking into why these failed in your case. We will email you when we have found out what happened.

You told us in your email that these glasses are needed urgently for a wedding present, so we have packed another box and will send it by courier to your work address in Edinburgh today. It will arrive by 4.30pm at the latest.

We hope that this will make up for your earlier disappointment, and look forward to have you shopping with us again in the future.

Yours sincerely

Julie Brown
Customer Services Manager
julie.brown@glassesforyou.com
www.glassesforyou.com
0171 888 888

GLASSES
FOR YOU

Emails and letters

Writing letters to customers

Here are some key points:

- Your letter needs a structure – a clear beginning, middle and end – to help the reader digest the information quickly and easily.

- Don't over-punctuate. You don't need full stops in the date or in the name or commas in the address.

- The date is usually written as 7 April 2012 rather than 7th April 2012.

- Use 'Dear Mr, Mrs, Miss or Ms' unless you are on first-name terms with the reader. If you don't know the reader's name, then use 'Dear Sir' or 'Dear Madam'.

- You usually start a letter with 'Thank you for your letter of 7 April'. If you use 'I acknowledge receipt of' or 'Further to your recent' you can come over as stuffy and old-fashioned.

- If you think a heading is necessary, then use bold rather than capitals. Don't use 're:'.

- If you started the letter with 'Dear Mr, Mrs, Miss, Ms, Sir or Madam' then end it with 'Yours faithfully'. If you started the letter with 'Dear Sue' then end it with 'Yours sincerely'.

Good practice

- Include your contact details in case the reader wants to get back in touch with you.
- **Always** check over the letter before you send it.

Example of a letter to a customer.

Julie Brown
Customer Services Manager
Glasses For You
Bankhead Industrial Estate
Aberford AD12 6FG
21 July 2012

Mr J Smith
Company Offices
Brown and Brown Ltd
High Street
Aberford AD11 1FH

Dear Mr Smith

Delivery of broken crystal glasses

I emailed you this morning to apologise for the fact that three of the six crystal glasses you ordered from our website were broken on arrival.

You should receive this letter from the courier who is delivering another box of glasses to you at your work address. Please open the box and inspect the glasses to make sure that they are undamaged. I have asked the courier to wait until you have checked them, although I am sure that they will arrive in pristine condition.

As promised, we are currently looking into why the breakages happened in the first place. I will email you as soon as I know what happened. In the meantime, because you are a valued customer, please accept a voucher for £15 to make up for our mistake.

Please contact me if you have any other issues you would like to discuss. I am here to help.

Yours faithfully
Julie Brown
Customer Services Manager
julie.brown@glassesforyou.com
www.glassesforyou.com
0171 888 888

GLASSES
FOR YOU

Julie Brown
Customer Services Manager
Glasses For You
Bankhead Industrial Estate
Aberford AD12 6FG
21 July 2012

Mr J Smith
Company Offices
Brown and Brown Ltd
High Street
Aberford AD11 1FH

Dear Mr Smith

Delivery of broken crystal glasses

I emailed you this morning to apologise for the fact that three of the six crystal glasses you ordered from our website
were broken on arrival.

You should receive this letter from the courier who is delivering another box of glasses to you at your work address.
Please open the box and inspect the glasses to make sure that they are undamaged. I have asked the courier to wait until
you have checked them, although I am sure that they will arrive in pristine condition!

As promised, we are currently looking into why the breakages happened in the first place. I will email you as soon as I
know what happened. In the meantime, because you are a valued customer, please accept a voucher for £15 to make up
for our mistake.

Please contact me if you have any other issues you would like to discuss. I am here to help.

Yours faithfully

Julie Brown

Julie Brown
Customer Services Manager
julie.brown@glassesforyou.com
www.glassesforyou.com
0171 888 888

REPORTS

The thought of having to write a business report can be very intimidating to some people. But don't worry – it's not difficult. Half of the battle is remembering and applying the principles of plain English, and we've already covered that.

What we are going to focus on here is the process involved in writing a report, and the way it is organised and structured.

The process of writing a report

Like all types of writing, there is a process for writing a report. And, as with other types of writing, you can repeat parts of this process until you are happy with your report. It will help you to focus your thoughts and give you somewhere to start.

Here's the suggested process:

- **Define the purpose of your report.** Why are you writing it and who are your readers?
- **Research the information you need.** This will depend on the type of report you are writing. You might need to devise a questionnaire, interview people, use the internet or look in

company records or accounts. Ask the person who has asked you to do the report for help, if you need it.

- **Plan and structure.** This will help you to make sense of all the information you have gathered, and help you to produce an organised, clear and concise report.
- **Write your first draft.** Do a rough draft – don't worry too much about how it looks at this stage – and it will give you a good idea of how your report is shaping up.
- **Revise and edit.** Refer back to Chapter 2 for advice.
- **Identify any missing information.** Revising and editing your writing usually reveals any gaps that need to be filled.
- **Cut out what you don't need.** The editing process also reveals what you don't need.
- **Write the final draft.** Give it to a critical friend to look over.

Planning your report

You need to plan your report if you want it to be well-organised, clear and concise.

Reports

Imagine that you work for your local government education department. Your boss has asked you to write a report about the impact of music projects on junior and senior schools in Goldenvalley. This is to inform senior management about whether to continue funding music in local schools.

You have defined the purpose of the report, and you have gathered the information you need by devising different questionnaires and interviewing different groups of people. You have also read music guidelines and policy documents.

Now it's time to plan it. Here's a suggestion for how you can do this.

You'll probably have gathered a lot of information, so mind mapping can help you to empty your head of that information, then sort it out.

- Get a piece of paper and write down all your ideas – don't worry about perfect writing at this point – just get the content down.
- Get a clean piece of paper. Put the topic box in the middle of the page.
- Now think about the main ideas of your report – what are they?

Structuring your report

- Draw lines from the topic box to these main ideas.
- Now add information where you think it sits within these main ideas.
- Make links between the main ideas.

There is an example of a mind map on the next page.

Structuring your report

Once you've got your plan worked out, it's time to structure the report. Here's an example of a structure you could use – most reports follow this model.

- Title/title page
- Contents
- Executive summary
- Introduction
- Findings
- Summary and conclusions
- Recommendations
- Appendix

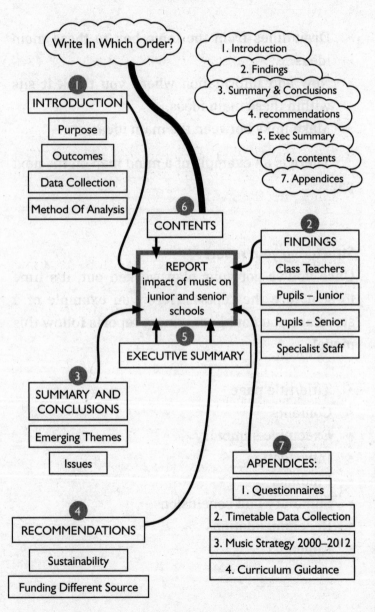

Write In Which Order?

1. Introduction
2. Findings
3. Summary & Conclusions
4. recommendations
5. Exec Summary
6. contents
7. Appendices

1 INTRODUCTION
- Purpose
- Outcomes
- Data Collection
- Method Of Analysis

6 CONTENTS

2 FINDINGS
- Class Teachers
- Pupils – Junior
- Pupils – Senior
- Specialist Staff

REPORT
impact of music on junior and senior schools

5 EXECUTIVE SUMMARY

3 SUMMARY AND CONCLUSIONS
- Emerging Themes
- Issues

7 APPENDICES:
- 1. Questionnaires
- 2. Timetable Data Collection
- 3. Music Strategy 2000–2012
- 4. Curriculum Guidance

4 RECOMMENDATIONS
- Sustainability
- Funding Different Source

Sections within the structure

Let's look at what each of these sections involves in more detail.

Title page

A short report only needs a title. A long report needs a title page. On the next page there is an example of a title page.

Contents page

A long report needs a contents page. A short report doesn't.

Here's an example of a contents page:

Contents

Executive summary
Introduction
Purpose
Outcomes
Data collection
Method of analysis

Findings
Class teachers

REPORT

THE IMPACT OF MUSIC ON JUNIOR AND SENIOR SCHOOLS IN GOLDENVALLEY

Anne Other

Education advisor
Goldenvalley Education Department

JANUARY 2013

Sections within the structure

Pupils in junior schools

Pupils in senior schools

Specialist staff

Summary and conclusions

Emerging themes

Issues

Recommendations

Sustainability

Funding

Appendices

Appendix 1 Questionnaires

Appendix 2 Timetable for collection of data

Appendix 3 Copy of *Music Strategy for 2000–2012*

Appendix 4 Curriculum Guidance Goldenvalley Education Department

Executive summary

This is a summarised version of the summary, conclusions and recommendations of the report. It means that people can get the overall picture without having to plough through the whole report. The executive summary is often circulated as a separate document because it saves people time and money.

Here's an example of an executive summary:

Executive summary

A number of conclusions, issues and recommendations have emerged from this report.

Conclusions
- All music projects have a very positive impact on the pupils and staff involved.
- The music projects all support the Goldenvalley Curriculum Guidance.
- Access to music is as wide as possible within age constraints, and all projects are inclusive.
- Teachers are more confident about taking up professional development in music and trying out new music activities themselves in the classroom.
- The music specialist team is strong and provides a valuable service.
- Many of the music projects have given pupils access to musical experiences that they wouldn't otherwise have had.

Issues
- Should funding be continued?

Sections within the structure

- Long term sustainability needs to be discussed.

Recommendations

- Set up a new fund for music projects – there is evidence to prove that music benefits all of the stakeholders in junior and senior schools.
- Solve the issue of long-term sustainability by funding a programme of professional development for classroom teachers, supported by the music specialist team and learning and teaching packs.

Introduction

The introduction should be clear and concise. It should answer the following questions:

- What is the report about?
- Who asked for the report and why?
- What is the background to the report?
- What was your method of working and collecting data?

Here is an example of an introduction:

Introduction

This report was requested by the Senior Management Team of Goldenvalley Education Department. The aim of this report is to:

Reports

- evaluate the impact of music projects on junior and senior schools in Goldenvalley
- recommend whether or not to continue funding these projects.

The music projects were previously funded by education department money. However, cuts have to be made in local government spending, and each curriculum area is being evaluated to assess how essential it is for pupils' education.

Data for the report was collected by the following methods:

- questionnaires, followed up by interview
- observation
- reading reports.

Four different questionnaires were devised (for junior pupils, senior pupils, teachers and music specialists) and used to gather data.

The questionnaires asked for qualitative responses only. In most cases, respondents were asked to fill out the form before the interview. If they had any questions or were unclear about any of the questions, they could bring this up during the interview.

The main part of this report – the section on 'Findings' – records and analyses respondents' views of music projects in junior and senior schools. All interviews

Sections within the structure

were carried out face-to-face using the questionnaires in Appendix 1.

All other sources used for this report are also in the Appendices section.

Findings

This is the main body of the report. It will be the longest section, because it will expand on your Executive Summary, and it will contain all the detailed information that you have gathered and analysed.

Remember to write concisely and clearly, and apply plain English principles. Organise your work under headings and subheadings.

The findings for Goldenvalley Education Department will be organised as follows:

Findings

Class teachers

This section will explore the impact that the music projects have had on classroom teachers.

[The report will then go on to **cite**, **analyse** and **interpret** the qualitative and quantitative evidence for this group of respondents.]

Pupils in junior schools

This section will explore the impact that the music projects have had on pupils in junior schools.

[The report will then go on to **cite**, **analyse** and **interpret** the qualitative and quantitative evidence for this group of respondents.]

Pupils in senior schools

This section will explore the impact that the music projects have had on pupils in senior schools.

[The report will then go on to **cite**, **analyse** and **interpret** the qualitative and quantitative evidence for this group of respondents.]

Specialist staff

This section will explore the impact that the music projects have had on specialist staff who teach music.

[The report will then go on to **cite**, **analyse** and **interpret** the qualitative and quantitative evidence for this group of respondents.]

Summary and conclusions

The summary and conclusions section describes the purpose of the report, what your conclusions are and how you reached them. Again, keep this section clear and concise.

Sections within the structure

Here is an example:

Summary and conclusions

A number of points have emerged from this report.

All the music projects have had a very positive impact on the pupils and staff involved. They have, without exception, developed pupils' confidence and self-esteem, and have developed their overall performance. The projects are about achievement as well as attainment.

The in-school projects have managed to get over the 'If I can't play a musical instrument, I can't teach music' syndrome amongst classroom teachers. Teachers are more confident about taking up opportunities in music and trying out new activities themselves. This has been largely due to support from either music specialists or from learning and teaching support packs.

The music specialist team is strong, and provides a musical service.

Many of the projects have given pupils the opportunity to have musical experiences that they would not otherwise have had. These pupils will take these experiences with them throughout their lives.

The main issue that has emerged is the sustainability of funding. The music projects were previously funded by education department money. However, cuts have to be

Reports

made in local government spending, and each curriculum area is being evaluated to assess how essential it is for pupils' education. The question is how essential is music to pupils' overall education and personal development compared to other subjects?

Recommendations

Your main findings or conclusions will lead to your recommendations. What issues do you think have emerged from your findings and what actions or options do you recommend to address them?

Again, keep this section brief and to the point. Many people reading the report will go straight to this section, because it's the one that really matters.

Recommendations

The findings from the report suggest that music has had a beneficial impact on both pupils and staff. Music has helped to develop pupils' learning as well as their personal and social development, and this report therefore recommends that music should continue to be taught in junior and senior schools in Goldenvalley.

However, the major issue is that music has always been funded centrally, and that savings must be made in

Sections within the structure

this central budget. The following two suggestions could help to resolve these issues:

- Divert some of the culture and heritage lottery funding to schools with the justification that they are educating the concert- and theatre-goers of tomorrow – if there are no audiences to play to, there will be no concerts.

- Solve the issue of long-term sustainability by using some of these funds to develop a programme of professional development for classroom teachers, supported by the music specialist team and learning and teaching packs.

Appendix

If you have generated a lot of research material, such as charts, tables, questionnaires or statistics, then put these in an appendix/appendices, or they will disrupt the flow of the report.

Here is an example of what the appendices could contain:

Appendices

Appendix 1: Questionnaires

Appendix 2: Timetable for data collection

Appendix 3: Copy of *Music Strategy 2000–2012*

Appendix 4: Curriculum Guidance for junior and senior schools in Goldenvalley

Staying relevant, objective and factual

As with all writing, when you are writing a long report, it is very important that you stay relevant throughout or you will lose the reader's concentration and understanding (and goodwill). A good, well-planned structure will help you to stay on track and develop a logical, concise and clear argument.

When you are writing a report, you also need to be objective and factual. You are not writing a personal note or a letter to the local newspaper – you have been asked to review all the facts objectively, assess the evidence and come up with recommendations based on this.

Remember to keep your tone formal and neutral, with no inappropriate jokes or asides. Apply the principles of plain English and keep in mind the purpose of the report all the time you are researching and writing it.

PRESENTATIONS

Many of us will have to make a presentation at work at some point in our working lives – either as part of an interview when we are applying for a job, or as a regular part of our job. It's an effective way to communicate information to a group of people. Many people break out in a cold sweat just thinking about it, but there's really no need. Follow these tips and you will be writing and giving polished, professional and confident presentations.

There is also an example of a PowerPoint presentation at the end of this section.

Planning a presentation

As with any other type of writing, it's important to plan your presentation first.

There are four things you need to consider before you put pen to paper or touch your keyboard:

- purpose
- audience
- venue
- remit.

Presentations

Purpose

What's the purpose of your presentation? What do you want the audience to know and remember about it? Once you have decided that, you can then go on to decide the most appropriate tone and style. For example, a presentation to a job interview panel would be formal and conservative, whereas a presentation to a media company for sponsorship would probably be much more creative and informal.

Audience

Who is your audience? What do they know about your topic? What are your audience's needs and how can you meet them? For example, if they are members of an interview panel, they will want to know about your previous experience and ability to carry out the job. If they are members of a media company you are asking for sponsorship, they will want to know about who you are, what you are going to do with the money they give you and what they are going to get out of it.

Venue

Where are you making your presentation? Is it in a small, intimate room or a large hall? What kind of atmosphere are you trying to create? Will this venue affect your relationship with your audience? If it affects this negatively, can you change the venue to suit your needs?

Remit

A remit is slightly different from the purpose of the presentation. For example, somebody in your company might have asked you to make a presentation to a particular group using a specific template – and you have to stick to this.

Make sure that you are clear about the remit, and have all the rules and guidelines that you need before you start working on the presentation.

Structuring a presentation

A presentation should be clear, concise and logical. Don't get tangled up in complex structures. You need to explain and discuss your points clearly. Here is a suggested structure for a presentation:

- Introduction
- Main points (linked together logically and coherently)
- Conclusion.

Introduction

This is where you must gain the audience's interest and confidence. Wait until your audience is quiet, and then begin speaking with energy and enthusiasm.

Here are some key points in an effective introduction:

- **introduce yourself**
  'Hello, my name is Anne Other ...'

- **say what you are going to be talking about**
  '... and I am going to be talking about how my business can help yours.'

- **say how you are going to approach the topic**
  'I am going to describe my background, what I write and how my writing services could help your business.'

- **say what the outcome of the presentation is going to be**
  'I hope that as a result of my presentation, you will choose my company to write your marketing and promotional materials.'

- **tell the audience what they need to do**
  'At the end of my presentation I will take any questions.'

Structuring a presentation

Main points (linked together logically and coherently)
These form the biggest part of your presentation. Here are some key points to help you develop this section:

- List the main points you want to make. What are you trying to tell your audience? What do you want them to learn?
- Think about the logical sequence for these points – think of this as a story – then put your points in this order.
- Now add supporting information and any diagrams or illustrations you think would be helpful.
- Keep it clear and concise, and always use plain English.
- Please be careful about using humour. People can interpret jokes so differently, and what one person finds funny, another might find offensive. Best to leave it out, unless your remit is to be a stand-up comedian.

Conclusion
Audiences remember the first and last things you say, so make an impact on your audience with a

strong and effective conclusion. Summarise the purpose and content of your presentation, and reinforce the outcome.

Here are some key points in an effective conclusion:

- **reinforce the purpose and content**

  'This presentation has described what I write and how my writing services could help your business.'

- **say what your conclusions are**

  'I think that I have the experience and expertise to write your marketing and promotional materials.'

- **say what you would like the next stages to be**

  'I would like to talk in more detail about the type of marketing and promotional materials you need.'

- **say what is going to happen next**

  'I am happy to take any questions you have.'

- **thank your audience**

  'Thank you very much for giving me the chance to pitch for this work.'

Delivering an effective presentation

When you are making a presentation, you are also giving a performance – or acting. The audience responds to you in the same way they would to any

Delivering an effective presentation

performance, so you need to think about how you use your voice and your body.

Here are some key points to help you deliver an effective presentation performance:

- Remember that practice makes perfect.
- Use body language, posture, eye contact and gestures.
- Use your voice.
- Breathe.
- Be enthusiastic and energetic.
- Be prepared.

Remember that practice makes perfect

Remember that delivering a presentation is really a performance, and that actors rehearse before a performance. It makes sense to practise your presentation before you make it. In fact, find an empty room, stand up and make your presentation. How did you perform? What do you need to improve or work on? The more familiar you are with your presentation, the more comfortable and confident you'll be delivering it.

Use body language

You don't just communicate with your voice. Your

body can also say a lot about what you are thinking and feeling. So be aware of this and use it to your advantage.

First of all, think about your **posture.** If you cross your arms and hunch your shoulders, you will immediately give the impression that you are defensive and nervous. Stand up tall, with your shoulders back. This will not only make you look more confident and self-assured – it will help you to breathe better and to project your voice more easily.

You need to make **eye contact** with your audience. If you don't, they won't feel that you are interested in them or that they are involved in your presentation. If you have a small audience, make eye contact with all the members. If you have a large audience, you obviously won't be able to make eye contact with every individual, so focus on different points around the room. This will make it look as if you are involving everybody. Don't look at the floor or ceiling – this will come across as if you are bored or being rude.

People use **gestures** all the time to emphasise a point or to help them describe something, so use gestures in your presentation, too. It would look a bit odd if you just stood there with your arms stuck to your sides. Open your arms as a welcoming gesture, and make gestures to emphasise points or show you have finished.

Keep the gestures open, moving away from your body and towards your audience. This will help to make the audience feel included, and will help to break down any barriers.

On the other hand, however, be careful not to use too many gestures, and don't gesticulate wildly – this will make you look nervous and unprofessional, and it will probably distract your audience rather than make them listen to you.

Use your voice

The way you use your voice can make or break an effective presentation. You need to think about the volume at which you speak, the speed of your delivery and the pitch of your voice.

Your voice needs to be loud enough for the audience to hear, but if it's too loud, then it can be distracting. Use loud and soft to add some colour and interest to your delivery. Monotone is very boring.

If you speak too quickly, the audience won't be able to understand you, but if you speak too slowly, they will probably fall asleep. As with volume, vary the pace of your delivery to add some energy and interest.

The pitch of your voice varies in normal conversation. For example, if you are asking a question the pitch of your voice automatically rises. If you are giving someone a row, the pitch becomes lower.

Pitch is a useful tool to use in a presentation. Vary your pitch – try this out when you are practising your presentation. Remember that you are giving a performance.

Delivering an effective presentation

Breathe!

Many actors know the value of controlling their breathing. If you breathe steadily and deeply, this will calm your nerves and help you to control your voice. If you are nervous your breathing becomes fast and shallow, and this will make it more difficult to speak clearly and steadily.

Take a few deep breaths before you begin the presentation, and try to get into a steady breathing pattern.

Be enthusiastic and energetic

Show the audience that you are enthusiastic about your topic. If your presentation has a sense of energy, your audience will be more likely to feel interested and involved. If you are negative, lacking in energy and unenthusiastic, they won't engage with you.

Be prepared!

Presentations can fail because you haven't checked everything out beforehand. Disaster can happen, for example, if you haven't made sure that your equipment works or the room has been booked.

Presentations

It pays to do the following before your presentation:

- revise and edit your presentation to make sure you haven't made any mistakes
- rehearse on your own in the room, hall or theatre where you are making your presentation to get a sense of what it's like
- make sure the room, hall or theatre has been booked and is available on that day
- check the technology is working and that you have backup – just in case
- turn off your mobile phone.

What type of visual aid?

There are lots of different types of visual aids to help you make your presentation. Here are the most popular (in alphabetical order).

Flipchart

A flipchart is a large pad of paper on a metal stand. People usually write on a flipchart with coloured pens as they go through their presentation, although you could also prepare some sheets containing key points beforehand. You should write down one idea per sheet, otherwise it could get too

What type of visual aid?

cluttered for the audience to see clearly. You can flip backwards and forwards through the sheets to make and reinforce your points. Make sure your writing is clear and large enough to read from a distance, and don't draw over-complicated illustrations or diagrams.

Handout

Handouts are very handy. They give your audience a full record of your presentation which they can take away and digest in their own time. However, the issue is when is the best time to hand out your handout? If you give them out at the beginning or during the middle of your presentation, the audience might look at them and not listen to you. If you hand them out at the end, they might have already made lots of unnecessary notes – and this can be very annoying. One way to solve this could be to say at the beginning of the presentation that you are going to pass round a handout at the end, so the audience can concentrate on listening without having to make notes.

OHP

An overhead projector (OHP) and OHP slides or transparencies are particularly popular in education institutions. The OHP is a device that enlarges and projects transparencies onto a screen, whiteboard or a wall.

There are three ways to produce your transparencies:

- write or draw them yourself using either cleanable or permanent pens, or produce them on a computer **before the presentation**
- write them **during the presentation** using cleanable or permanent pens to record your points and feedback from the audience
- a bit of both.

What type of visual aid?

As with a flipchart, make sure that your writing is clear and large enough for the audience to read. If you are producing your text for the transparencies on computer, use 18 point text. Stick to one main idea per transparency, and don't draw overcomplicated illustrations or diagrams, because these can be distracting.

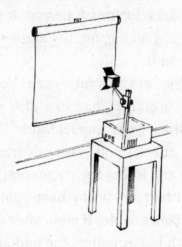

PowerPoint

The visual aid that most people now use is Microsoft PowerPoint. But beware, you need to know how to use it effectively – if you don't, your audience will get bored and restless. It's not a good sign when you hear whispers, sweet papers rustling or pens tapping. But that's not going to happen to you, because here are some key points to producing a successful PowerPoint presentation:

- Use a font that the audience can read – at least 20pt. If the text is too small, then the audience won't be able to read it. Can the people at the back see it?
- Keep the background as simple as possible. If you introduce too much design, it will conflict with the text and again, the audience won't be able to read it.
- Animations are useful when you want to illustrate a point. They can also inject some interest into your presentation. But if you overuse them, you risk distracting your audience and losing their attention.
- Vary your text and try to make your slides look clean and accessible. If slide after slide is peppered with bullet points, the audience will get bored and their attention will wander.

Video

A little bit of video can go a long way – so use it carefully. Like animation, it can inject interest into your presentation, but too much is distracting.

What type of visual aid?

Whiteboard

A whiteboard is a large board that you can write on and then rub off. It is useful for presenting processes, a sequence of ideas, events or stages involved in scientific experiments. Many scientists use whiteboards in their presentations for this reason.

You can write the title of or key points of each stage of the experiment or process on the board, along with essential references. Make sure that your audience has noted everything they need before you wipe it off, though. And make sure that your writing or diagrams are clear and large enough for your audience to read.

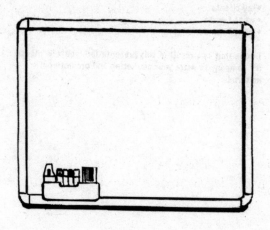

Example of a PowerPoint presentation

Here is an example of a PowerPoint presentation.

The person making this presentation wants to persuade the company that she can write their marketing and promotional materials.

INTRODUCTION

My name is Anne Other, the owner of Word Solutions.

I am going to talk about how my writing services could help your business by discussing:

• my approach
• my clients
• what I write
• what I can do for you

I hope that as a result of this presentation, you will choose my company to write your marketing and promotional materials.

Example of a PowerPoint presentation

Word Solutions
~For All Your Writing Needs

MY APPROACH

Choosing the right words is essential in life, but particularly so in business.

Words can give the right – or wrong – impression to your customers.

I write to a wide variety of briefs. I listen carefully to what you want, so you actually get what you want.

Word Solutions
~For All Your Writing Needs

MY CLIENTS

My clients come from the following sectors ...

• commerce
• industry
• banking
• education
• local government
• charity sector

... so I have experience in writing lots of different types of marketing and promotional materials.

WHAT I WRITE

Most of my work is in the following categories, although I always enjoy a new challenge:

- **marketing and promotional materials**
- **websites**
- **learning and teaching materials**
- **reports, research studies and case studies**
- **news articles/features**
- **rewriting/editing**

WHAT I CAN DO FOR YOU

I have written lots of different types of marketing and promotional materials for lots of different businesses.

I have the experience and expertise to help you.

I use a tried and tested process that gives my clients exactly what they want:

- You tell me what you're looking for. If my quote is acceptable, we form a team.
- We discuss your brief. We can do this at a face-to-face meeting, by using Skype or phone or by email – it's up to you.
- I write a first draft.
- We discuss this, and I edit it until you are happy with the final product.

Example of a PowerPoint presentation

CONCLUSION

How can Word Solutions help your business?

- experience and expertise to write high quality marketing and promotional materials
- one-to-one discussion about your project
- we recognise that you are unique and interpret your brief accordingly
- professional marketing materials are more likely to get you noticed

Questions welcome!

Thank you for your time.

CONTACT DETAILS

Anne Other
The Cottage
Elm Street
Goldenvalley
GO13 7AN

telephone:	01337 888 888
mobile:	07777 999999
email:	anne.other@wordsolutions.co.uk

MARKETING AND PROMOTIONAL WRITING

If you are involved in writing marketing or promotional materials, then you need to know about copywriting.

You write copy (or text) to advertise or market/sell a product, business, opinion or idea. Copy is written for marketing and promotional materials such as:

- adverts (including TV, radio, newspaper, magazine and billboard)
- brochures/leaflets
- websites
- press releases
- social media

You will probably only ever need to write copy for a brochure/leaflet or website, because adverts and press releases are fairly specialised, and are usually handled by a press or advertising agency.

Let's look at the general approach to copywriting, then concentrate on how to write copy for brochures/leaflets and websites.

General approach

The main thing to remember is that your copy is selling a product, business, opinion or idea to somebody.

Audience

It is therefore vital to know who your audience is, how much they know about your product, business, opinion or idea, and what you want to persuade them to do (or not do!). For example, you might want to persuade somebody to buy a yacht, or to stop eating junk food and start eating healthily.

Style and tone

So how do you make your copy persuasive? You will have to vary your approach, depending on your audience. The person buying the yacht will probably need a different approach to the person you want to eat healthily.

A good rule of thumb is to make your copy memorable or unusual in some way, so that it holds people's attention. This is a good opportunity to express yourself. You are not describing the process involved in filling out a tax return. Be creative. Think of a hook you can use to draw people in. Look at other marketing and promotional materials to see the tone and style they use to engage the reader.

Call to action

And whatever it is you are persuading your audience to do, you need to ask (or tell) them to do it at the end of your copy. This is what is known as a 'call to action', and it should be concise, punchy and clear. Let's use the yacht and healthy eating examples again:

> So if you want to sail off happily into the sunset, phone 0121 222333.

> Junk food out. Healthy food in. Visit our website (www.eatinghealthily.com) and send for our free healthy eating pack. Today!

Writing brochures/leaflets

You might have to write copy for a product or service that your company is selling. This could take the form of a brochure or leaflet that the company mails or gives out to visitors. Or it could be an e-leaflet.

Writing brochures/leaflets

Whatever the format, it's important to use powerful and compelling headlines to get the reader interested enough to find out more. Think of an unusual metaphor or ploy to attract your audience. The main body of the copy should then expand and build on this headline, and finish with a call to action – for example, an invitation to phone or visit the website.

Example of a leaflet

Here's an example of a leaflet. Its purpose is to sell a software training package called TrainIT.

A brain teaser and a no-brainer

Grab a cup of coffee and take two minutes to unscramble these two sentences. (Here's a clue – they're about saving your business money.)

> training your Is profits? draining
>
> the answer e-leaflet is yes, If read this
>
> solution. for the

Worked it out yet? If not, go back and have a second cup of coffee. Got it? Good. We're going to tell you how you can stop training draining your hard-earned profits.

The solution lies in an award winning software package called TrainIT. It's been created and produced by a company

Marketing and promotional writing

called SmartIT – a technology leader and trendsetter.
TrainIT has four key cost- and time-saving features:

1. It enables you to develop your **own** library of training materials inhouse at a pace that suits you and your staff.

2. As a result, staff won't have to travel to expensive training seminars, with consequent loss of time at work – they can use the training materials on-site and at a time that suits them.

3. The software can create training materials that suit the unique needs of **your** business and **your** staff – unlike external training, which is often too general to be relevant.

4. You can go back and edit and update the training materials as often as you want – so staff don't have to go on endless training updates every time a new version of software comes out.

The reason you can do all this is because the techie types at SmartIT have come up with a nifty thing called 'capture technology'. Here's how it works.

Imagine that you are in charge of IT training and that you want to explain to a new employee how to create a PowerPoint presentation.

Writing brochures/leaflets

You go through the process of creating a PowerPoint yourself on screen, and as you do this, each step of the process is captured and written down. You can then add your own specific instructions using an audio narrative function. You can also create speech bubbles and 'post-it' notes that will appear on the file and give the user extra support.

Once you've finished working through the process, you save it and create a 'smartlearn' file that you can add to your training library. Staff can then use this file to view and listen to the process, interact with the process or test their knowledge of the process. There is (of course) an initial cost but the long term advantage is that you'll have a reduction of up to 80 per cent in training time and costs.*

If it all sounds too good to be true, it's not. We know because we use the software ourselves. And what we've described are only the basic functions.

But please don't take our word for it – phone us on 0777 888999 and we'll arrange a demonstration so that you can understand the power and implications of TrainIT for yourself.

*you think When it about, no-brainer. it's of a bit a

SmartIT
High Street
Aberford AD11 1QZ
0777 888999

Writing for websites

You only have a few seconds to grab someone's attention when they visit a website. If you don't, they will move onto another, more interesting one. Here are some tips to help your copy stand out.

Presenting information

People don't read web pages the same way they read printed material – they tend to scan and jump about the page rather than read from left to right, and from top to bottom. You therefore need to think about the following:

- Make your sentences and paragraphs **short and concise** to help **scanning** and **skimming.**
- Use **different levels** and **fonts** in your **subheadings** to signpost specific pieces of information.
- Use **bulleted lists** to break up the text.
- Make sure there is plenty of **blank space** around your text – this helps text to stand out and makes it easier to read.
- **Limit** the amount of text per page.

Here's an example of the type of concise text that tells you immediately about the business:

Writing for websites

Front Door Apartments

Welcome to Front Door Apartments. We offer boutique, serviced apartments in charming Stockbridge, ten minutes' walk from Edinburgh's West End. We specialise in luxury accommodation at non-luxury prices for anything from one night to three months – whatever your reason for visiting Edinburgh.

Our apartments are special. They combine the boutique chic of a city hotel with the freedom and flexibility to allow you to explore this beautiful city at your leisure.

Browse our website to find out what's on offer.

Our philosophy at Front Door Apartments is to provide the highest levels of service, with little extras like local insider information that will make your stay more special.

Writing content

Again, readers won't approach a web page in the way they do a printed page. So you need to approach website copywriting in a different way. Think about the following:

- Users want to know immediately where they are, so use big, clear page headings.
- Write bite-size chunks of copy, not big portions.

- There should only be one topic per page. If you need to include more information, then create a downloadable file (such as a pdf) and put it on your page.

- Put the most important piece of information at the top of the page. Have a look at a newspaper – this is what they do.

Plain English

Writing plain English is even more important in this context. Your copy can be seen by anybody anywhere in the world and reading too much text on a screen gives you sore eyes. Keep it short, sharp and concise.

Go back to the section on plain English in Chapter 2 to remind yourself of the principles.

Here are links to some websites that illustrate some of the features we have discussed:

BBC

The website for BBC news, sport, TV, radio and education materials.

www.bbc.co.uk

The Guardian
The website for *The Guardian* newspaper featuring news, sport, comment, analysis and reviews.

www.guardian.co.uk

WWF's Earth Hour
The website for information about WWF's Earth Hour is an example of a website with clear headings and concise text.

http://earthhour.wwf.org.uk

Social media
Many organisations now use social media to market and promote themselves. They encourage readers to share and pass on their information within social networks such as Facebook and Twitter. It's basically marketing by word of mouth, it's fast, very effective and it costs very little. It's also becoming more popular: recent statistics show that 57 per cent of small businesses use social media. These companies give various reasons, among them promoting awareness of their company, boosting sales, improving customer ser-

vice and search engine optimization. Its use as a marketing tool is unsurprising when you look at the increasing use of social media. In 2011, social media and blogs accounted for nearly a quarter of the time people spent on the internet, with 4 out of 5 visiting these types of websites. Surveys also show that 53 per cent of adult social media users follow at least one brand account.

However, if you are asked to do this kind of copywriting, be careful. Remember that you are still representing your organisation. Don't be lured into thinking that you can write in an inappropriate style and tone or make inflammatory comments just because you are writing for a social network. Stick to the standards expected by your company, and apply the same principles that you would to writing copy for any other medium.

Besides this, there are a few key things to bear in mind when writing for social media on behalf of a company:

- **Research**. Just like with any other form of writing for business, planning is key to writing for social media – don't just leap right into your first post. Research the different sites out

Writing for websites

there before you do anything else – should you use Facebook, Twitter, LinkedIn, Pinterest, Google+, a blog, or a combination? They all have different audiences and formats. Find the one which is most suitable for your purposes and then speak directly to that audience.

- **Plan and proof**. Once you've chosen, you need to devise a strategy for using that particular format. How often will you post? What will you post? Social media needs to be updated regularly to be of any use, and this needs to be factored in from the beginning. Having plans for future posts, or constructing a library of posts, can be useful.

  Social media clients such as HootSuite (http://hootsuite.com/) and TweetDeck (http://tweetdeck.com/) also allow you to post and monitor activity on major social media sites, as well as to schedule updates. Once you start writing posts, planning is still crucial. A sense of spontaneity is good in social media, but it is also a danger. Consider what you're writing: posting without thinking is not a good idea from business accounts. As said before, professionalism still needs to be maintained in this medium.

Marketing and promotional writing

Writing too quickly can also look unprofessional if you aren't taking the time to proof what you've written. Sloppy spelling and punctuation will look just as bad in this format as any other, and using text speak (for example to accommodate Twitter word limits) will still make your writing unprofessional and hard to understand.

Follow plain English rules, and bear in mind that it's very easy to post, but very hard to take back when you have.

- **Contribute**. It is important, not just to post regularly, but to post high quality content. If you use social media just to post links to your website, or to say how well the company is doing, readers are simply not going to be engaged. Think outside the box: what will allow readers to get to know your business while still being interesting?

Remember, not all things that are of interest to those inside the company will be of interest to readers on social media. Consider company news, links to blog posts, videos, tips, posts by different staff members. Whatever you choose to write, always bear your audience in mind when writing content. You can't rely on the idea that this audience will read and respond to anything you post: they will only read and share what interests and engages them.

Remember that social media is not just about communicating to the widest audience possible, but about providing something valuable to those who follow you.

- **Be social**. It seems obvious to say, but social media is, above all, social. It doesn't work merely to set up a profile and create posts, and expect a loyal following to appear. You need to commit time and energy to providing interesting content, building up relationships, and engaging directly with subscribers. Always talk 'with' on social media, don't just talk 'at'.

- **Communicate**. When people follow or subscribe to companies on social media, they expect a direct line to these companies. Especially on more informal sites like Twitter and Facebook, this is an opportunity to show a business's human face.

Allowing customers to talk to a human voice, with a personality, is what makes social media so different from the more distanced voice of other forms of communication. This voice should also be a natural one – don't try to manufacture a voice for the company, just be yourself.

This aspect of social media makes it all the more important, however, to keep appropriateness and professionalism in mind during all communication with followers. Don't be tempted to over-share.

- **Respond**. Inviting people to communicate with you, which is what you are doing when you join social media, means that you have to listen and respond to what they say. Respond to feedback. Acknowledge and deal with complaints, as you would if you received them via any other medium, in a polite, efficient way. Communicating with customers in the public eye in this way makes this professionalism just as, if not more, important than if they were contacting you in any other way.

- **Adapt**. Social media is changing all the time, so it is especially important to monitor what you are doing, and to adapt strategies accordingly. Sites like Klout (klout.com), an online influence indicator, can help in this.

Writing for websites

It is also important to adapt style depending on which type of social media you are using. LinkedIn, for example, would require a more formal style than Twitter or Facebook, where informality is preferable.

- **Commit**. Above all, successfully writing for social media takes commitment. Invest time and effort, be interested in and communicative with others and give it time, and eventually you will build up a loyal following.

WRITING ANNOUNCEMENTS

Most organisations have to make regular announcements about important changes – either good or bad. Some have guidelines for such announcements. However, some give managers the responsibility for producing these. You might be asked to write such an announcement, so it's important to know how to go about it.

We'll look at the general approach to writing an announcement for both good and bad news and include an example of each.

Writing announcements

General approach

As with most pieces of writing, there should be a distinct beginning, middle and end to an announcement. Here are some general points that you can apply to all announcements.

Get your facts correct

What change is the organisation announcing? A new employee, a promotion, redundancy plans, a retirement, a new policy or a company event? Before you write anything, make sure that you have got facts such as names, dates and times correct.

Presentation style

This depends on how you are sending out your announcement.

If it's by email, then use the standard email format for your organisation, and insert a concise but clear title in the 'subject' section so that readers will immediately know what the announcement is about.

If you are putting a notice on the staff notice board, the format could be something like this:

General approach

To:	All staff
From:	Senior management team
Date:	7 April 2012
Subject:	Notice of change

Write the main body of your announcement first. This will probably take two or three paragraphs.

Once you are finished your announcement, make sure you include a contact name and number so that staff can get back to you if they have any queries, like this:

If you have any queries about this announcement, please contact Joe Bloggs on extension 2222.

Beginning: tell the news straight away

State what the announcement is about in the first sentence:

We are delighted to inform you that Eleanor Rigby has joined the company as a junior member of the human resources team.

or

We are sad to inform you that Eleanor Rigby, Head of Human Resources, has decided to retire after 30 years' service with the organisation.

Writing announcements

Middle: develop the news

Develop the story of what led to this change over the next few sentences:

> Eleanor joined the HR team straight from university. For Eleanor, HR is a passion. She worked hard and was promoted several times until she reached the post of Head of Human Resources. She leaves behind her a well-organised, efficient and effective department, and we will all miss her.

End: looking forward and being positive

The announcement should end on a positive note, with employees looking to the future rather than to the past. It should also flag up any events associated with the news.

> We hope that Eleanor enjoys spending more time on her other passion – playing her violin. She is welcome to come in and serenade us any time! We are holding a leaving event for Eleanor on 15 December – everyone is welcome to come and say goodbye. Mince pies and mulled wine are on the menu!

General approach

Style and tone

Engage or talk to your readers by using 'you' and 'we', but remember that you are representing the company – so your style and tone should be clear, concise, polite and objective.

Example of an announcement

So here's what the final notice would look like:

To:	All staff
From:	Senior management team
Date:	7 April 2012
Subject:	Eleanor Rigby retires

We are sad to inform you that Eleanor Rigby, Head of Human Resources, has decided to retire after 30 years' service with the organisation.

    Eleanor joined the HR team straight from university. For Eleanor, HR is a passion. She worked hard and was promoted several times until she reached the post of Head of Human Resources. She leaves behind her a well-organised, efficient and effective department, and we will all miss her.

We hope that Eleanor enjoys spending more time on her other passion – playing her violin. She is welcome to come in and serenade us any time! She will also have more time to spend with her family, friends and her four beloved grandchildren. We heard on the grapevine (well, from the HR department, actually!) that she is giving up one career to take up another, as a part-time childminder.

We are holding a leaving event for Eleanor on 15 December – everyone is welcome to come and say goodbye. Mince pies and mulled wine are on the menu!

If you want to make a contribution to her leaving present, please contact Paul McCaster on extension 2468.

How to announce good news

It's probably easier to announce good news because you know that everyone will want to read about it.

Your tone and style can be more informal in this context, and you might even want to include some humour.

Example of how to announce good news

Here's an example of this type of announcement:

From:	Senior management team
To:	All staff
Date:	7 April 2012
Subject:	Good news!

How to announce bad news

We have just heard that we have won the huge contract to produce recycled brown paper bags for all the GoodFood supermarkets in Europe!

The senior management team worked day and night to plan and produce a convincing case for this pitch. They were invited to present their pitch along with ten other shortlisted companies at the GoodFood headquarters in Brussels last week. We got the good news this morning.

This means a major expansion for our company. We will be recruiting 50 new members of staff to deal with the extra work. They will mainly be in the production and distribution side, and we are hoping to start advertising and interviewing for the posts as soon as possible. Details of the contract will be posted on the company website today.

Tea and buns in the staff room at 3pm to celebrate!

How to announce bad news

Writing about bad news can be a bit more difficult. Most companies will have an HR department to deal with announcements about redundancies or major staffing changes.

However, you might have to fire or dismiss a member of staff and then tell other staff about this. This could cause quite a shock, so you need to be logical and factual – not emotional. You also need to be sure about what you can and can't say in this situation.

After the employee who has been dismissed has left the building, and a staff meeting has been held to tell employees about this and to inform them of changes to their duties, etc., you can follow up with an announcement – either by email, or on the staff notice board, or both.

Example of how to announce bad news

Here's an example of this type of announcement:

From: Manager, Production Department

To: All staff

Date: 20 September 2010

Subject: Termination of employment: James
               Brown

I am writing to let you know that James Brown, Project Manager in the Production Department, no longer works for this organisation.

James Brown's projects will be covered in the short term by the other five members of the Production Department, until we have advertised and filled his post.

How to announce bad news

Because of reasons of confidentiality, I am unable to discuss the details of this termination of employment. However, I am happy to discuss how we plan to share out roles and responsibilities across the other members of the team. My extension number is 2468.

I am sure that we will all pull together, as always, to keep the production department working effectively and efficiently until we have recruited a new Project Manager.

WRITING FOR THE MEDIA

INTRODUCTION

We all talk about the media, but what do we really mean by it? Here's one definition:

> **media:** a means of reaching many people, such as through television, newspapers and radio.

The media includes:

- newspapers
- magazines
- TV and radio
- the internet

In this chapter, we are going to look at what makes writing for the media different from other types of writing. We will also focus on the different types of media available, and the different styles required by these. So we hope you find this helpful, whether you are a budding young newspaper or TV journalist, or you just want to know how to write a newsletter for your football club.

WHAT'S UNIQUE ABOUT WRITING FOR THE MEDIA?

When you are writing for the media, you don't necessarily have the captive audience that you do when you are writing an academic essay or a work email. You have to grab your reader's attention, because you are competing with lots of other news features, articles, TV/radio programmes or blogs. Readers are like butterflies – they will flit from one piece of information to another. So how do you grab their attention and keep it? We are going to look at the following techniques to help you do this:

- who, what, how, where, when and why (the five Ws and an H)
- media style
- interviewing techniques
- house style
- 'spin'

The five Ws and an H

- **Who** is involved?
- **What** happened?
- **How** did it happen?
- **Where** did it happen?
- **When** did it happen?
- **Why** did it happen?

These are the time-honoured questions that journalists and media writers use to structure their writing. First, you grab the reader's attention by creating a strong, dramatic introduction for maximum impact, and then you use the 'five Ws and an H' structure keep their attention by providing the answers to these questions.

Example of 'five Ws and an H'

Here's an example of a news report that uses this structure to describe Raisin Weekend – a traditional event that takes place every year at St Andrews University in Scotland.

Raisin Weekend high jinks at St Andrews (Introduction)

Despite the freezing cold yesterday, hundreds of students

What's unique about writing for the media?

at St Andrews University took part in a foam fight in St Salvator's Quadrangle, marking the end of the annual Raisin Weekend celebrations.

(Who)

This is a university tradition where new students – known as bejants and bejantines – are adopted and shown the ropes by an academic 'mother' and 'father', who are usually third-year students.

(What)

On the Sunday of Raisin Weekend, the 'parents' throw a party to help all their 'children' get to know each other. This is usually helped along by copious amounts of alcohol.

As a thank-you present, the children give their parents a bottle of wine – it used to be a pound of raisins. Academic fathers acknowledge this gift by giving their children a raisin 'receipt'. This was originally written in Latin on a piece of parchment, but now it's written on an object that the student has to push or drag to the foam fight on Raisin Monday. And the mothers – as all good mothers do – dress their children up for the event.

Raisin receipts and costumes can be anything – the more outrageous and embarrassing the better. This year,

The five Ws and an H

one student was spotted pulling an old iron bedstead along behind him, wearing only a nappy.

(How)

So how did this crazy tradition start? Nobody seems quite clear. Some people think it's only a century old, while others believe that it goes right back to the fifteenth century.

(Where)

Whatever its origins, Raisin Weekend creates mayhem in St Andrews, and this can sometimes cause tension between 'town' and 'gown'. A Tesco employee grumbled: 'I don't mind a bit of high jinks, but some of them are drunk and cause trouble in the shop. One student stole a couple of items. The police have been in and out all day!' But the majority of the residents and visitors take it as a bit of a joke. Elinor Hay who was on holiday from Glasgow, said: 'I've just seen a young lad stark naked on top of the fountain in Market Street! I've not seen a gorgeous young body like that for twenty years – I went back for another look!'

Joe Brown, the President of the Student's Union, commented: 'It's a great experience, and one that St Andrews graduates always remember. The combination

What's unique about writing for the media?

of foam, grass and frost will always remind me of my first year at St Andrews. And the local pubs and hotels do a roaring trade, so it's a win-win situation.'

(When)

Raisin Weekend takes place on the Sunday and Monday of the second weekend in November every year.

(Why)

The aim of this tradition is to help new students integrate into university life. Perhaps that's when William and Kate got to know each other better ...

Media style

Newspapers, magazines, websites and blogs are not textbooks – they communicate information to readers who are probably on their way to or from work, or are catching up on the news during their lunch hour. They don't have time to read the same sentence over three times because they don't understand it. And if they don't like what they're reading, they'll skip it and go to something else. So it's back to plain English again – media style is crisp, concise, easy to understand – but also colourful and enjoyable to read. You'll be competing

Media style

with other news items, articles or columns, so your opening has to hook the reader in and make them want to read on. The 'five Ws and an H' help with this, but establishing your own style or voice is important too.

Example of two openings

Compare these two openings, for example – which one is more likely to make you want to read on?

Opening A

Emily Dickinson was an American poet who lived from 1830–1886. She spent most of her life living in her family homestead in Amherst, Massachusetts – a town that still had a very Puritan culture. Her father, Edward Dickinson, was treasurer of Amherst College for nearly forty years, as well as being a lawyer and politician. Emily never married, but wrote prolifically, especially between the years 1861–1865. In 1862, she averaged a poem a day.

By the time of her death, she had written some eighteen hundred poems, though even her family didn't know how many poems she'd written. Only around ten of her poems were published in her own lifetime, and she died unknown as a poet. Instead, she collected and sewed her poems into carefully crafted 'fascicles', and

What's unique about writing for the media?

stowed them away. From the 1860s, Dickinson had begun to withdraw from town life, and to dress entirely in white. Around 1869, when she was thirty-eight, Emily chose to stay permanently within the family's home and grounds, never going beyond them. Her sister Lavinia discovered all of Emily's poems when she died and, along with Mabel Loomis Todd, a neighbour, helped to publish them. A complete version of her works was only made available in 1955. Until then, versions of her poems available were often not very true to the original and made changes to her punctuation and style.

Opening B

'The Homestead', in the centre of Amherst, Massachusetts, is an impressive brick structure built in the Federal style. Upstairs, in a simply-furnished bedroom on the upper left of the house, a small writing desk – around 16 inches square – sits in the corner-room's angle. The modest reality of this desk belies the importance of its former owner, who, during nights spent sitting before it, poured out a truly prolific body of poetry, and then put it away unseen in its drawers.

Emily Dickinson wrote some eighteen hundred poems before her death in 1886. She lived for almost her entire life in The Homestead, her family home, and,

Media style

despite her reputation today, died almost unknown as a poet beyond its walls. Even her sister Lavinia, who knew of her writing, was surprised to discover, after Emily's death, the volume of work locked in her desk.

Emily's work came, for her innumerable fans, terrifyingly close to never seeing the light of day. But how could a writer of such genius have died with only around ten of her poems having ever been published? And why did the woman, famed in the public consciousness as a recluse dressed all in white, choose to confine herself in later life to the family grounds; to turn herself almost into a living-myth?

The answer to this may lie in considering Emily not just as a poet, but as a female poet. It's hard to imagine today that Emily's work could go unlauded during her lifetime, but the situation for a woman writer, much less one as uncompromising and challenging as Emily, was entirely different in the Puritanical landscape of 19th century New England. Woman writers during this period were stretching the traditional boundaries of what females were allowed to do in a very real way. Only a generation before, women writers were just about unheard of, and publication (the act of being made public) would be considered shameful for any woman — whose role was exclusively in the domestic sphere. Even

What's unique about writing for the media?

in Emily's day, the freedom to write, especially full time as she did, was hard-won.

Opening A fails to reveal the focus of the article, and you are none the wiser by the end of the paragraph. Is this a history of Emily Dickinson's life? Is it a feature on people who became recluses? Or is it about women writers in 19th-century America? It's difficult to tell. The writing is bland, with no structure or punch and there isn't much of a hook to persuade the reader to persevere. Opening B sets an engaging scene and draws the reader in by asking interesting questions. The focus of the article is then introduced, the reader mentally goes 'Aaah, I see' and settles down to find out more about the difficulties faced by American women writers in a culture where women were perceived as belonging only in the domestic sphere.

Interviewing techniques

If you are writing for the media, then you'll need to interview people. Interviews are a good way of gathering facts, opinions and stories from people. Quotations give your writing vitality and human interest, and they make it unique to you.

Interviewing techniques

But how do you develop interviewing techniques? To begin with, you need the following qualities:

- persistence
- curiosity
- patience
- confidence
- empathy
- sensitivity
- enthusiasm.

If you interview somebody and you want them to open up to you, then you need to make eye contact, use friendly and open body language and look interested. They're not going to engage with you if you come over as cold, bored or uncaring.

The following techniques will help you to carry out efficient and professional interviews.

Do your research

Find out everything you can about who you are going to interview – this will help you to feel confident and ask the right questions.

What's unique about writing for the media?

Plan and structure

What information are you trying to get? Plan the questions and structure of your interview to make sure that you get this information. You can always move away from this structure from time to time if a new idea or issue turns up, but you have the structure to return to.

Establish a rapport

You need to establish a rapport with the person you are interviewing, so it helps to be professional, businesslike, friendly, courteous and polite.

Ask open-ended questions

Phrase your questions carefully. If you ask closed questions – questions that only need a 'yes' or a 'no' answer – then the interviewee won't have a chance to open up to you. So instead of asking 'Do you like the publicity that comes with your job?' ask 'What do you think about the publicity that comes with your job?'

House style

Would you refer to the 1939–45 war as World War 2, World War II or the Second World War? Or how

House style

would you refer to the years 1980 to 1989 – the Eighties, eighties, 80s or '80s? Is it organise or organize?

We all have our own preferences for words, phrases and spellings, but if we followed them it would be confusing for the reader, so most serious newspapers, magazines and media websites have what is known as a house style. This ensures that there is a uniform approach to the language used by writers and editors.

Example of house style

Here's an example from a publishing house style guide:

captions

In general, captions do not need a full point afterwards.

Short captions look odd and old-fashioned with a full point afterwards – omit the full point.

Mixture of long and short captions – omit final point on all of them. In an informal text this is especially true.

In a more formal or technical text, with captions made up of several sentences, a full point at the end will probably look better. Use common sense.

What's unique about writing for the media?

caster sugar

Caster rather than castor. Both are right, however caster appears more often on modern packaging.

centuries

The 20th century, the 21st century. Hyphenate when adjectival, e.g. 21st-century boy.

20th Century Fox doesn't hyphenate its name, leave it be if it is mentioned.

colon

Within a sentence, don't follow a colon with a capital. Usually the first word following a colon looks better uncapitalised. However, if a full sentence follows the colon it will probably look better to cap up the first letter of that sentence.

In some display styles, it may look better to capitalise the first letter of the first word following the colon. Keep it consistent whatever's chosen.

> Here are some examples of how we've used colons:
> *Arm discs: Also known as Delphin discs, arm discs are available in adult and child sizes. These are the modern take on inflatable arm bands.*

House style

Before you get in the water:
Blow your nose. You should not swim with
a cold or with catarrh.

Keep going until you have gone a few
metres, then try moving in different
directions: sideways, backwards and in
circles.

commas

Try to avoid lots of unnecessary commas. Commas are used for parenthesis, lists and to avoid ambiguity not to indicate lots of pauses, which is very old fashioned.

company names

Companies and institutions are singular (the Bank of Scotland is, the school is, Vauxhall is, the government is).

Many company names have apostrophes in them: if in doubt, check the official website.

cross references

See pages 122–23. Italicise 'See/see' and always have the word 'page' written out in full, *not* p. or pg.

Most page references will be appearing in brackets. Put bracketed page reference inside an existing sentence.

What's unique about writing for the media?

Use an en dash between page references and shorten when there is repetition of the first numbers as follows:

123–4 *not* 123–24 or 123–124

23–4 *not* 23–24

267–79

267–345

Check out the *The Guardian Style Guide* on www.guardian.co.uk/styleguide/.

Ask to see the house style book or sheet of the newspaper, magazine or website you are writing for. Some might only be a page of A4, with very basic guidance, while others cover every question that a writer or editor is likely to ask. Most house styles will cover the following:

Preferred dictionary

Most media organisations tend to have a preferred dictionary that they use. These could include:

- *The Oxford Dictionary*
- *Cambridge Dictionary*
- *Chambers Dictionary*
- *Collins Dictionary*

House style

The house style will probably state whether to use '-ise' or '-ize' verb endings.

Addresses, ages, dates and numbers

There will probably be rules to cover how you write addresses, a person's age, dates and cash amounts.

Most newspapers and magazines spell out numbers one to ten in full, but use figures for 11 and over.

Collective nouns

It's now generally accepted that most collective nouns use a single verb, as in the following:

The music society is charging a higher fee.
The government is deciding on the best policy.

There are some common exceptions, and these include the police, pop groups and football teams:

The police are asking for help to solve the crime.
The Rolling Stones are performing for one last time.
Manchester United are playing well just now.

What's unique about writing for the media?

Hyphens and en rules

Do you co-operate or cooperate? Co-ordinate or coordinate? Write Stratford-upon-Avon or Stratford upon Avon? House rules will tell you what to do.

Don't confuse hyphens with en rules or em rules. These are used – like this – in parenthetical statements. Some organisations prefer to use the en rule – like this. It's the width of a capital 'N'. Others prefer to use an em rule — like this. It's the width of a capital 'M'.

Abbreviations, titles, capital letters and royalty

There will probably be a section on abbreviations in most house styles – for example, ie or i.e.?

Titles might be punctuated – for example, Dr., Mr. and Prof.. But names might not be – for example, JK Rowling.

There will be a style for when to use capital letters – too many can make a line or heading difficult to read.

There will also be a style for addressing royalty – for example, HRH, HM, Her Royal Highness or Her Majesty.

Spin

Fonts and layouts

Finally, some media organisations will also state the fonts and layouts they prefer.

Style of language

We'll look at style of language in more detail in the next section.

Spin

Spin is associated with the media, but what exactly is it?

One view of spin is that it is a way of presenting news or an incident to your audience to persuade them to see it from a particular perspective – usually to reduce the negative impact. So instead of saying, 'We failed 20 per cent of our targets' you would say 'We met 80 per cent of our targets'. Or, instead of writing 'I failed this term's chemistry test' you would say 'I am learning from the mistakes I made in this chemistry test to help me achieve a top mark in my next test.' You are turning a negative into a positive.

Spin is used a lot by public relations people in politics and the media. Often, when a celebrity makes a mistake or does something embarrassing, they employ a public relations officer to put a spin on events and lessen the impact. Some people therefore think that 'spin' and 'spin doctors' – the people who use spin – are manipulative and are not to be trusted.

If you use spin, you must consider the ethics involved. There are two different ways to look at it.

One view is that if you basically tell the truth but put a spin on it, then if the reader doesn't ask questions or think about what you have written, that's their fault and not yours.

The other view is that you are intentionally trying to control the way the reader interprets the facts by making them look at them in a more positive light.

Be careful about where, when and how much you use spin. Think of the purpose of your writing – is spin appropriate for your readers? If not, keep things simple and don't use it.

Look out for examples of spin when you are reading or listening to anything in the media.

DIFFERENT MEDIA, DIFFERENT STYLES

In this section, we'll look at the styles required for different types of media. We will cover the following:

- newspapers: tabloids and broadsheets
- magazines
- feature writing
- ezines
- newsletters
- blogs and websites
- reviews

We will also look again at the issue of copyright in the context of writing for the media.

Newspapers

There are two different types of newspapers – tabloids and broadsheets. They look different, have a different style of writing and aim to attract different readers.

On the next page is a summary of the main differences:

Different media, different styles

Tabloids and broadsheets

Tabloid	**Broadsheet**
The Sun, Mail, Mirror	*The Times, Guardian, Telegraph*
'popular' approach	more serious, analytical approach
bold layout	more conservative layout, more
focus on photographs	focus on text
sensational headlines	factual headlines
language biased and emotional	language more objective
focus on stories about	focus on major world events
famous people, gossip and	and politics
sensational events	

Examples of tabloid and broadsheet headlines

A young man has been killed in a road traffic accident. Compare the different headlines written by the tabloid and broadsheet newspapers.

Tabloid headline

Village devastated by tragic death of car-smash victim.

Broadsheet headline

Local youth killed in tragic road accident.

Newspapers

Examples of tabloid and broadsheet report approach

Tabloid news report approach

A whole village is in mourning today for the loss of a 'well-loved' young man, who was a popular member of the community.

Justin Brown, 18, died tragically as a result of a head-on collision on his way to work yesterday. He had a promising career in front of him, and colleagues are still reeling from the news.

'We still can't get our heads round it,' said his boss, Jim Smith.

Police are still at a loss about what happened, and are asking for eyewitnesses to come forward with information.

Broadsheet news report approach

A local youth who had just embarked on an engineering apprenticeship was killed yesterday in a tragic head-on collision on his way to work.

Family, friends and colleagues were devastated by the news.

A representative of the local police said 'We would appeal to any eyewitnesses to come forward with information so we can identify the cause of the accident.'

We've looked at the differences between the two main types of newspapers. Now we're going to look at the common aspects of the structure and style of a newspaper article. Refer back to the 'Raisin Weekend high jinks at St Andrews' article (*see* page 183) when you are looking at these points.

Structure and style

- The headline has to be punchy and eye-catching. It has to catch people's attention and make them want to read the article.
- Always keep the 'five Ws and an H' in mind – this should be your structure for every article.
- Each paragraph should clearly link to the next.
- Tell the story, and tell it in chronological order.
- Include quotations to add human interest, authenticity and life to your writing.
- Include official sources of information where appropriate – for example, police, local authorities, the person in charge.
- Try to finish on a forward-looking note, even if it is bad news.

Magazines

There are magazines on just about every topic

Magazines

under the sun from fly-fishing to women's interests to buying a car. Magazines have a different
writing style and pace from newspapers. They
have feature articles rather than news stories, and
their readers buy the magazine because they want
to read these features.

Here are some of the types of features that you
will find in magazines:

News features

These are linked to stories in the news. They usually explore the story in more depth, or look at it
from a fresh angle.

Profiles

One-to-one interviews are very popular in magazines, and can range from celebrities to ordinary
people with an interesting story to tell.

Lifestyle features

How do you juggle being a working mum? What
do you do at the weekend? Where do you shop
and what do you cook? These are all the subject of
popular lifestyle features.

Consumer features

These involve comparing and assessing rival products, so you the reader don't have to.

Question and answer

This is a common interview structure, where the person being interviewed simply answers a list of published questions. The writer just records the answers without interpreting or analysing them.

Specialist features

These require specialist knowledge because they deal with specialist subjects such as antiques, travel or motoring, for example.

We've looked at the different types of feature articles you will find in magazines. Now we're going to look at the structure and style of this type of writing.

Structure and style

- Your introduction still needs to have impact and you still need to answer the 'five Ws and an H' in your feature, but not at the pace of a news story.
- Decide what your angle is going to be. Stay

Magazines

focused and relevant to this angle – plan where you are going before you start writing. This will help your writing to flow and will stop you losing your way.

- End with a bang, not a whimper! Try to create a well-rounded ending.
- Make sure that you have a good mixture of facts, quotes and your own observations/interpretations of places and people.
- Put your ideas in a logical progression, so that the feature flows.
- Avoid repetition and 'purple prose', but use imaginative language.
- Think about your tone – is it appropriate?

Example of a feature profile

Here is an example of a feature profile. It's a one-to-one interview with a lady who remembers growing up during the Second World War.

Yesterday's girl

The Oscar-winning film *The King's Speech* well and truly pushed the country's nostalgia button. Google it and you get over 70 million results. But does the film reflect what life was like for yesterday's ordinary boys and girls?

Different media, different styles

Maureen Forrester (74) gives us an insight by describing her memories of growing up during the reign of George VI in the 40s and 50s.

Cupar is a market town in north east Fife, and Maureen Forrester was born and grew up there during the war. She has strong memories of the Polish soldiers who were billeted in the area. Apparently they were very polite, with lots of heel-clicking and hand-kissing. And most thrilling of all, they had chocolate.

Maureen said: 'We had two Polish soldiers billeted with us. I had such a lovely time because I was only three and they made a big fuss of me. They brought us bars of chocolate, which you hardly ever saw. That was a great treat. Crowds of them would come up to our house – not just the ones staying with us – and my mother would play the piano and we would all have a sing song. It was just wonderful!'

'Of course,' she added, 'it goes without saying that the Scottish men were very jealous of the chocolate-giving and the hand-kissing. They didn't like the competition at all!'

Maureen remembers a strong sense of family and community during the war. Her sister joined the Land Army, and Maureen went to stay with her one weekend on a farm in the north of Fife. She said: 'I was out working in the fields with all the girls, and we had such a great

Magazines

laugh. It was great! My mother made me trousers to wear, because girls didn't wear trousers then.'

Children were also expected to help out in the fields during the school holidays. Maureen described, laughing, what happened when they went to pick potatoes: 'We left home in the dark and made our way to a collection point. The farmers would arrive with open lorries and choose whom they wanted. We were loaded onto trucks with no notion of where we were going, then dumped in a field and set to work. Can you imagine children being treated like that nowadays? Either they'd be arguing with the farmer about their rights or their parents would.'

Sugar rationing also encouraged the community spirit. Maureen said: 'I remember putting a jam jar in the middle of the table and instead of putting sugar in our tea or on our cornflakes, we put it in the jar. When we had collected enough, we made tablet.'

However, since Maureen's father was in the motor trade and was responsible for rationing petrol, he often brought the family extra luxuries from grateful customers. He usually came back from visiting one particular farm laden with eggs. Maureen laughed: 'But the best gift that we ever got was a whole pig — not alive I have to say. We kept it in the garage!'

Different media, different styles

Like most of yesterday's girls and boys, Maureen and her sister were keen cyclists – so keen in fact, that they planned a cycling and hostelling trip to Norway when they were 16 and 20. She recalled: 'We cycled from Cupar to Newcastle, stopping at hostels on the way, and caught the ferry to Bergen.'

But this was no wild, cocktail-swigging holiday – quite the opposite. Maureen said, laughing: 'We were very prim and proper and kept ourselves to ourselves. In one hostel, some Norwegian men realised we were British and started to sing "I dream of Jeannie with the light brown hair". They were just trying to be friendly, but we were highly insulted and snubbed them!'

Thankfully, Maureen let her guard down enough for one Ron Forrester to woo and marry her 'at the tender age of 19'. Ron planned and organised a honeymoon to remember. She recalled: 'He was an adventurer. We drove from Cupar to Lydd in our little Morris Minor shooting brake. At the small airport there we boarded the plane, and our car was driven along with two others into the front of a Bristol Wayfarer. We landed at Le Touquet and then drove down through France, across the interior of Spain, over the Pyrenees to Andorra and back up through France on our way home again.'

Then it was back to earth with a bump. Like most women of her time, she decided to make marriage her career. But four children later, she decided that she wanted more out of life, and went back to college to study music. Maureen had always loved music and singing in particular. She said: 'When I was young, I would sing loudly in the garden, hoping that some Hollywood producer would just happen to be wandering down our little street, looking for another Shirley Temple!' After completing her course, she became a teacher, which also gave her the opportunity to produce and sing in musical shows. 'So it all worked out well in the end!'

Maureen still teaches piano to a small number of pupils, and as I get ready to leave, this yesterday's girl opens the door to one of tomorrow's young musicians.

Ezines

What is an ezine? It's an electronic magazine, delivered through email to people who subscribe to it. Ezines are usually free, and cover a huge amount of topics. They are therefore often used as a marketing tool. You can write an ezine article or your own ezine to lead potential customers to your business website.

Different media, different styles

Here are some tips for writing in this medium.

Research

Before you write your own ezine article, use any search engine and type in 'ezine publishers' to find out who is out there and what they are publishing. Once you know your market, you can write your article or develop your own ezine.

Write your article

Write your article in plain English. Refer back to the general approach to writing for the media at the beginning of this chapter. This is your chance to show your expertise, establish credibility and advertise your company or your own business.

Remember that if you submit an article or business information to an established ezine, your audience is subscribing to the ezine because they are interested in the topic that you are writing about. You're off to a winning start.

Resource box

Ezine publishers sometimes ask for a resource box to be included at the end of an article submission. If you want it, this is your big opportunity

Ezines

to advertise yourself, your business and your website. It should contain the following:

- your name
- business name
- call to action (*see* page 158)
- website address
- email address
- experience and qualifications

Every time your article is published, there will be a live link in this resource box that goes to your website. This in turn will help to improve the search engine ranking of your website, especially if you use important keywords.

Developing your own ezine

If you want to create your own ezine, follow the same principles as above. You can then either add your ezine to an existing directory or list of publishers, or email existing clients and ask them to subscribe. After that, it's up to you how often you write and publish your ezine.

Example of an ezine

There are lots of examples of ezines on the

internet. Use any search engine to look for ezine lists or directories. On the next page is a spread from *Cake Masters* ezine. This is an online publication that goes out of its way to support and encourage the cake baking community – both professionals and hobby bakers. Much of the content comes from their readers' contributions, in the form of text and photographs.

Promotion of an ezine goes hand in hand with embracing social media, and *Cake Masters* does this enthusiastically. *Cake Masters*' Facebook page is a great example of how to use Facebook effectively: it is helpful, informative and entertaining, has just the right tone of informality, never posts anything controversial or argumentative, and it engages with and replies to its users and shares their content too. These users are, after all, potential readers of, and even contributors to, the magazine.

Some ezines are free, and some are available subscription or payment only. Others might give a free taster to encourage the reader to take out a subscription or make a payment per edition. The *Cake Masters* ezine's popularity as an online magazine has encouraged the editors to start selling their online edition for a payment and also

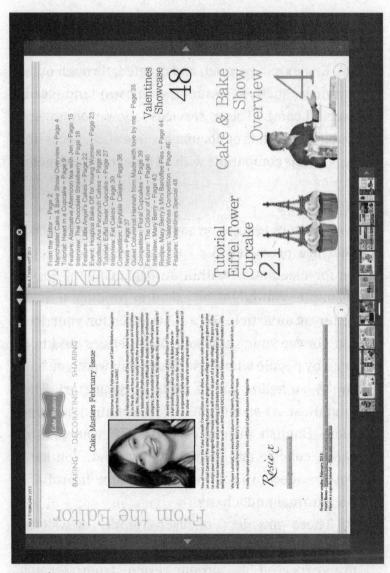

Extract from *issuu.com/cakemasters* online magazine.

producing a print edition for sale by mail from their website.

Ezines can be read, and created, through online services such as **issuu (issuu.com)** and **scribd (scribd.com).** These services allow you to self-publish all kinds of documents in a slick, accessible way that is compatible with all types of social media.

Newsletters

Newsletters tend to be short, printed publications that are produced for specific groups of people, or for circulation within an organisation. So, for example, you might be asked to produce a newsletter or an article for a newsletter for your local club or for your staffroom. Newsletters tend to be read by people who are interested in what you have to say, so again, you're off to a flying start. They contain short sound-bites of information, so apply plain English principles and keep your writing short, concise and easy to understand. You know your readers, so the tone and style will probably be informal and 'chatty'.

There are lots of user-friendly newsletter templates available on the internet if you are expected to produce one from scratch.

Alternatively, the organisation or group you are writing for could already have a template that they use, and all you have to do is to produce the articles to fit in it.

The Littleby Orchestral Society NEWSLETTER

EDITORIAL

Hello and welcome to the February edition of the Littleby Orchestral Society newsletter, where we look back at our Christmas concert and look forward to our next performance at the local spring festival. We've also got some lovely news about one of our players and a special offer for sheet music – so take some time out of your busy day, read and enjoy!

January concert

Congratulations to everyone who played in the Christmas concert – it was a sellout! Despite the cold and snow, friends, family and music lovers came in their droves to listen to our programme of Christmas carols, music from 'The Snowman' and Corelli's Christmas Concerto. We even got an encore!

The local press gave us a good review, so here's hoping the next concert will be as successful. The money will help us to hire the venue and sheet music for our spring festival performance.

SPRING FESTIVAL PERFORMANCE

Music has been chosen and rehearsals begin next Tuesday at 7.30pm in the school dining hall as usual. We are playing the 'Simple Symphony' by Benjamin Britten and 'The Planets' by Gustav Holst. To round off the British Composers theme we are performing 'The Lark Ascending' by Vaughan Williams.

A NEW ADDITION TO THE ORCHESTRA?

Jane Smith, our first horn player, is certainly doing her bit to generate new players for the orchestra. She and her family are celebrating the birth of twins Tom and Sarah. We are all thinking of you, Jane (and Tom!) and hope you don't have too many sleepless nights. Volunteers are available for lullaby playing!

SHEET MUSIC OFFER

Our local music shop, Green's Music, has offered Littleby Orchestral Society players a hefty 30 per cent discount on all sheet music for the month of February. So get down there now with your membership card and stock up on your favourites!

Different media, different styles

Blogs

The word 'blog' stands for 'web log'. A blog is a website that has entries (called posts) that appear in reverse chronological order (latest first). A blog is like an online journal or diary, where you write your thoughts or opinions about a subject. Blogs are now used for online journalism, because the writer can describe or record what is going on minute-by-minute – for example, at the Olympics or at the Oscars. Most blogs have an area where people can comment or respond to the blog post.

A blogger is someone who writes content for a blog, or posts a blog.

Why do you want to blog?

Before you go on to set up a blog, it's a good idea to ask yourself why you want to write a blog. That will focus your mind on the purpose of the blog, who your audience is going to be, how often you are going to post an entry and whether you are able to sustain it.

For example, is it to promote your business? In that case, you need to make it entertaining, with an unusual angle, not just a sales pitch. If it's about your view on international politics, then be careful

Blogs

not to let it degenerate into a rant. Remember that you want to build up a following for your chosen subject or field.

How to set up a blog

Once you've decided what you're going to blog about, there are lots of websites that offer free blogging. The most popular are WordPress, Blogger and Google. If you have a Google account, just log onto 'Blogger' and off you go. On other websites or blog platforms there is a 'create account' box where you enter your details.

You are then taken to a page where you have the option of allowing people to comment or respond. Write your post, click on the button to upload photographs or videos that you want to include and press the 'publish' button – you have posted your first blog!

Writing a blog

Follow the usual plain English rules – make it clear, concise and easy to understand. Short sentences are best. Don't ramble on with long sentences or you will lose your reader's interest. Remember your audience and keep focused.

If you mention the subject of your blog as often as you can in the first paragraph (without overdoing it), this will help your blog to feature prominently on the search engines. There is also a 'tag' section where you enter words that you want to associate with your blog. These will also help to push your blog up to the top of the list in search engines. Blogs vary very greatly in style, content, formality and approach. Some examples follow.

Examples of blogs

Cookery writer Jill Colonna has a blog called *Mad About Macarons* (madaboutmacarons.com) after her cookery book of the same name. Her blog is rather like a journal, with added recipes and descriptions of what it is like to be a British person living and working in Paris. Jill makes good use of social media with a very entertaining and active Facebook page where she takes time to reply to users.

She also engages with other writers in blogging communities such as FoodBuzz – essential if you want your blogging reputation to spread and your readership to grow.

Blogs

Home | Who's Jill? ▾ | About The Book ▾ | Bonus Recipes ▾ | Macaron Talk ▾ | Ask Jill ▾ | Boutique

Jour du Macaron — Macaron Day in Paris, 20 March 2012

by Jill on March 22, 2012 in Blog, Bonus Macarons, Loving France

Macaron Day may be over in Paris but it's time to relive the experience now that the last macaron is finished today from *le loot bag*.

A great gift for the 'macaronivore' in your life — 2nd edition out now!

Jill Colonna 2012

🇺🇸 Buy from amazon.com
🇬🇧 Buy from amazon.co.uk

Our sunny Paris macaronathon started out at Pierre Hermé's boutique at Opéra, with talented artist, Carol Gillott and clever 'Bear' of Paris Breakfasts fame. Where was the queue at 10h opening? There wasn't even time to wait in line and think about what first flavour to choose. Pressure. Many other boutiques were taking part in the Paris Jour du Macaron but as time was limited, we didn't manage to do all of them. However, we did well. Really well.

Never Miss a Blog Post

Enter your email address:

Subscribe
Delivered by FeedBurner

From *madaboutmacarons.com* written by Jill Colonna.

Writer Sue Reid Sexton is the author of *Mavis's Shoe*. Her blog entries at suereidsexton.blogspot. co.uk often talk about her life as a writer, and local writer events in which readers might be interested, but also, she often pays particular attention to the themes and locations that crop up in her novel.

It's a great way to help promote her book, because people searching for information on the Clydebank blitz (the setting for the novel) may well find Sue's blog and be encouraged to read her novel too.

Author of Mavis's Shoe, a novel about the Clydebank Blitz.

MONDAY, 11 MARCH 2013

'In what street?'

This is one of the saddest pictures I know of the aftermath of the Clydebank Blitz. I've put it here because Wednesday and Thursday of this week, the 13th and 14th March, will be the 72nd anniversary of the devastating bombing of Clydebank, the Clydebank Blitz. To mark this I'd like to talk about the numbers because since last year's anniversary I have discovered the source of those figures and the date. I was appalled, I have to admit, but subsequently greatly and sadly mystified.

The bombing shook Clydebank on a Thursday and a Friday. On the Sunday the authorities reported 528 dead, stating that there was 'probably a further 200'. Another 617 were said to have been seriously injured. This report was not made public at the time but these numbers were published the following year by the Sunday Post and the Sunday Mail. This was of course illegal because of war-time censorship and I believe the two papers got their knuckles rapped for their trouble.

The people of Clydebank are said to have been appalled by these numbers too. An ARP warden, who had been part of the rescue operation, is noted to have remarked on hearing the figures, 'In what street?' Eye-witness accounts confirm a far higher scale of damage and the sheer ratio of bombs and bombers to houses and people suggests the numbers were far higher: over 4,000 bombs for 12,000 dwellings. This is one bomb for every three houses. There were somewhere between 55,000 and 60,000 people living there, the population having swelled by 10 to 15 thousand because of the availability of war work.

But they don't know.

☑ Follow @SueReidSexton

• Sue's website

MAVIS'S SHOE AMAZON LINK

Order online

FOLLOWERS

Join this site
with Google Friend Connect

Members (11)

Already a member? Sign in

BLOG ARCHIVE

▼ 2013 (1)
  ▼ March (1)

From *suereidsexton.blogspot.co.uk* written by Sue Reid Sexton.

Journalist Tristan Stewart-Robertson has created a Canadian news site called *Tomorrow* (www.tomorrow.is) which is very much more formal than the sites previously mentioned. The articles are news features.

Tristan does not include any personal musings or opinions, or any facts that he has not checked numerous times and can give a citation for. On his site he has published an admirable list of guidelines and protocols that he feels are important for good reporting on his site and generally.

This is not really a blog, but it's an interesting contrast with the previous examples. *Tomorrow* is a content portal, and as it grows and finds new contributors it will look less a blog and more and more like a news site.

The ambitious ethical basis of the writing on this site is notable – and admirable – when in comparison to some blogs and 'news' writing on the web.

With very little digging you'll soon discover that many blogs contain unsubstantiated opinions and uncorroborated facts and information. They often contain photos and other content that breach copyright.

Different media, different styles

From *www.tomorrow.is* edited by Tristan Stewart-Robertson.

Of course there is room out there for personal opinions. Bloggers are the equivalent of the essayists of old – and that great tradition involves political comment, satire, humour and strong opinions. Even ranting, when done effectively, can be very entertaining. But it's important in this age – post Leveson Inquiry, where all the media are being scrutinised for ethics no matter what content – that you try to publish to a certain standard. A standard that, as a minimum, does not breach anyone's copyright, copy their work or ideas, do harm or spread unsubstantiated or uncorroborated information.

Reviews

An increasing number of people are writing reviews online on anything from cars to holidays to films, books and music. Some organisations like TripAdvisor actively encourage this, so that visitors to the site can make an informed decision based on honest opinions. You might want to contribute to a site like this after a particularly good (or bad) holiday. Or you might be asked to review a film or book for your organisation's internal newsletter, or want to do so for a personal blog.

Different media, different styles

So how would you go about doing this? What makes a good review? Here are a few points to remember.

What is the target audience/market?

If you know the target audience/market of the film, book or restaurant, you can judge it against a recognised set of criteria.

For example, a Hollywood action film and a low-budget art house film would appeal to completely different audiences, and you would therefore review them in different ways.

Include basic information

Make sure that you include basic information in your review such as:

- title, author, publisher and recommended price of a book
- title, director, main actors, cinema venue and times of a film
- name of restaurant, opening times and phone number for booking.

Reviews

Don't give away too much

Whet the reader's appetite by giving them enough information to let them decide whether they want to read the book or see the film, but don't spoil it by giving too much away.

Example of a review

Here is an example of a book review.

The Slap by Christos Tsiolkas

Christos Tsiolkas's fourth novel was longlisted for the Man Booker Prize 2010 and won the Commonwealth Writers' Prize, with good reason – it really makes you think.

The novel opens at a middle-class barbecue in Melbourne, Australia. It quickly builds up to the pivotal event – where a guest slaps a child who is not his – and then examines the fallout from the perspectives of the eight people who witnessed it.

Hector (Greek) and Aisha (Indian) are the affluent, middle-class hosts, Harry (Hector's hot-headed cousin) is the person who is responsible for 'the slap' and Hugh and Rosie (white, liberal and poor) are the parents of the slapped child. They report the matter to the police and take Harry to court.

Different media, different styles

But this novel is much more than the story of the events leading up to the court case, and its outcome. It forces us to examine our society and its issues, and in so doing it can sometimes make for uncomfortable reading.

Tsiolkas achieves this through the narratives of eight finely-drawn characters. Some, like Harry, are downright unlikeable, but are all the more convincing for that. They reveal their different deep-seated attitudes towards family, loyalty and race, and this in turn makes you question your own attitudes: for example, is it acceptable to hit an unruly child? Where would your loyalties lie – with the friend whose child was slapped or with your husband's brother, who did the slapping? How would you cope if your Greek wife was ashamed of your daughter-in-law because she was Indian?

These are difficult questions. Read this novel and ask yourself how you would answer them.

The Slap, by Christos Tsiolkas, is published by Atlantic Books. RRP is £7.99.

ACKNOWLEDGING SOURCES/COPYRIGHT

We've mentioned copyright before, but we're going to mention it again, because so many people think that if they use material from the internet that isn't actually on a printed page, they don't have to acknowledge it. This is just not true. You **must** identify all the material that is not your own – no matter what you are writing, where it comes from or what it is. If you copy **any** text, diagrams, photographs, art, music or web pages without acknowledging their source, then you are infringing copyright law, and could be prosecuted.

Copyright stays with the originator during his or her lifetime, and with the heirs to their estate for 70 years after their death.

WRITING CREATIVELY

INTRODUCTION

In this chapter we are going to concentrate on creative writing.

We will explain the characteristics of the two main types of prose fiction – short stories and novels – and will illustrate these with examples.

We will then examine the techniques that fiction writers use. This will help you to apply these techniques to your own compositions.

This chapter also examines the characteristics of some of the different non-fiction categories, including biographies, travel and cookery writing.

We will finally look at composition techniques for non-fiction writing.

FICTION

Fiction, or prose fiction as it is sometimes called,

tends to fall into two different categories – short stories and novels. Fiction means that the story is imaginary or made up – although many writers base their stories on something that has happened. Prose means that the story is written in sentences, paragraphs and chapters. It's not a play or a poem.

Short stories

Sometimes people think that a short story is a small novel. It's not. A short story is usually structured around a main conflict that happens near the beginning of the story, and sets the story in motion. We see the main character at this crucial point in their lives, where they have to deal with and resolve the events caused by this conflict.

There are lots of different types of short story, and no definite rules, but there are certain characteristics that all short stories have in common. A short story:

- tends to be less complex than a novel
- should be brief enough to read in a single sitting
- has a single plot
- has a single setting
- has a limited number of characters
- covers a short, or limited, period of time

Short stories

A short story also tends to have the following plot outline:

- There is an impactful, atmospheric opening.
- The main character(s) are introduced.
- The setting (time, place and relationships in the main character's life) is introduced.
- The problem/conflict the main character is facing is introduced and developed.
- The problem/conflict develops to a climax.
- This climax has a major effect on the character – for example, they acknowledge or come to understand something crucial, make a decision or take a course of action.
- There is a resolution – for example, the character deals in some way with the problem or conflict and there is a natural ending to the story.

Let's use a short story to illustrate these points. It's called *The Open Window* and it was written by H H Munro, otherwise known as Saki. Munro (1870–1916) was famous for writing short stories, and *The Open Window*, from *Beasts and Superbeasts* is one of his most popular. It is a story set within

Fiction

a story, and the open window of the title comes to symbolise how it can sometimes be difficult to distinguish between reality – or what we imagine to be reality – and appearances.

Impactful opening

Here's an example of an impactful, atmospheric opening, where we are thrown straight into an interesting and intriguing social scene:

> 'My aunt will be down presently, Mr Nuttel,' said a very self-possessed young lady of fifteen; 'in the meantime you must try and put up with me.'

The reader is immediately intrigued – who is Mr Nuttel, who is the self-possessed fifteen-year-old young lady, who is her aunt and what is the social context?

Introduction of main character(s)

Our curiosity is whetted even more when we are introduced, in Saki's inimitable humorous way, to the main character, the rather socially phobic Framton Nuttel:

Short stories

Framton Nuttel endeavoured to say the correct something which should duly flatter the niece of the moment without unduly discounting the aunt that was to come. Privately he doubted more than ever whether these formal visits on a succession of total strangers would do much towards helping the nerve cure which he was supposed to be undergoing.

Introduction of setting

Saki introduces and develops the setting over the next few paragraphs.

'I know how it will be,' his sister had said when he was preparing to migrate to this rural retreat; 'you will bury yourself down there and not speak to a living soul, and your nerves will be worse than ever from moping. I shall just give you letters of introduction to all the people I know there. Some of them, as far as I can remember, were quite nice.'

Framton wondered whether Mrs Sappleton, the lady to whom he was presenting one of the letters of introduction, came into the nice division.

'Do you know many of the people round here?' asked the niece, when she judged that they had had sufficient silent communion.

Fiction

'Hardly a soul,' said Framton. 'My sister was staying here, at the rectory, you know, some four years ago, and she gave me letters of introduction to some of the people here.'

He made the last statement in a tone of distinct regret.

'Then you know practically nothing about my aunt?' pursued the self-possessed young lady.

'Only her name and address,' admitted the caller. He was wondering whether Mrs Sappleton was in the married or widowed state. An undefinable something about the room seemed to suggest masculine habitation.

Problem/conflict introduced and developed

And then, devastatingly, the writer introduces and develops the conflict.

'Her great tragedy happened just three years ago,' said the child; 'that would be since your sister's time.'

'Her tragedy?' asked Framton; somehow in this restful country spot tragedies seemed out of place.

'You may wonder why we keep that window wide open on an October afternoon,' said the niece, indicating a large French window that opened onto a lawn.

'It is quite warm for the time of the year,' said

Short stories

Framton; 'but has that window got anything to do with the tragedy?'

'Out through that window, three years ago to a day, her husband and her two young brothers went off for their day's shooting. They never came back. In crossing the moor to their favourite snipe-shooting ground they were all three engulfed in a treacherous piece of bog. It had been that dreadful wet summer, you know, and places that were safe in other years gave way suddenly without warning. Their bodies were never recovered. That was the dreadful part of it.'

Here the child's voice lost its self-possessed note and became falteringly human. 'Poor aunt always thinks that they will come back someday, they and the little brown spaniel that was lost with them, and walk in at that window just as they used to do. That is why the window is kept open every evening till it is quite dusk. Poor dear aunt, she has often told me how they went out, her husband with his white waterproof coat over his arm, and Ronnie, her youngest brother, singing "Bertie, why do you bound?" as he always did to tease her, because she said it got on her nerves. Do you know, sometimes on still, quiet evenings like this, I almost get a creepy feeling that they will all walk in through that window –'

Problem/conflict develops to a climax
It's obvious that Nuttel believes this story, because when he meets Mrs Sappleton (the aunt) and she tells him that her husband and brothers will be home soon from snipe shooting, his reaction shows that he thinks she is insane:

> She rattled on cheerfully about the shooting and the scarcity of birds, and the prospects for duck in the winter. To Framton it was all purely horrible. He made a desperate but only partially successful effort to turn the talk onto a less ghastly topic, conscious that his hostess was giving him only a fragment of her attention and her eyes were constantly straying past him to the open window and the lawn beyond. It was certainly an unfortunate coincidence that he should have paid his visit on this tragic anniversary.
>
> 'The doctors agree in ordering me complete rest, an absence of mental excitement, and avoidance of anything in the nature of violent exercise,' announced Framton, who laboured under the tolerably widespread delusion that total strangers and chance acquaintances are hungry for the least detail of one's ailments and infirmities, their cause and cure.

Short stories

So Saki leads us brilliantly to the climax.

At this point, we believe like Nuttel that Mrs Sappleton is insane – her husband and brothers are dead and **won't** walk through the open window. So the next following three paragraphs have a powerful impact:

'Here they are at last!' she cried. 'Just in time for tea, and don't they look as if they were muddy up to the eyes!'

Framton shivered slightly and turned towards the niece with a look intended to convey sympathetic comprehension.

The child was starting out through the open window with a dazed horror in her eyes.

In a chill shock of nameless fear Framton swung round in his seat and looked in the same direction.

In the deepening twilight three figures were walking across the lawn towards the window; they all carried guns under their arms, and one of them was additionally burdened with a white coat hung over his shoulders. A tired brown spaniel kept close at their heels. Noiselessly they neared the house, and then a hoarse young voice chanted out of the dusk: 'I said, Bertie, why do you bound?'

Effect of this climax on the character

The effect on Framton Nuttel is immediate – he is scared out of his wits because as far as he is concerned he is seeing ghosts:

> Framton grabbed wildly at his stick and hat; the hall door, the gravel drive, and the front gate were dimly noted stages in his headlong retreat. A cyclist coming along the road had to run into the hedge to avoid imminent collision.

Resolution

The resolution is clever and unexpected, and takes the reader completely by surprise. The narrative is in the third person throughout, which means that the narrator portrays everybody's point of view, though as the story unfolds it's mostly Framton's thoughts and feelings we're given access to. Saki is really clever, because until Mr Nuttel runs out of the house and out of the story, we share his point of view, and we believe the story. But after he has run off, we stay in the house and find out that the open window was in fact the focus of a practical joke – a symbol of deception rather than a symbol of grief and unhappiness.

Short stories

Now we're in on the prank that Vera played on Nuttel, and she has played it on us too. The clues are scattered throughout that Vera has noticed Framton's nervous streak. It's only at this point that we realise that she was having some rather cruel fun with that failing. And it doesn't end there:

'Who was that who bolted out as we came up?'

'A most extraordinary man, a Mr Nuttel,' said Mrs Sappleton; 'could only talk about his illnesses, and dashed off without a word of goodbye or apology when you arrived. One would think he had seen a ghost.'

'I expect it was the spaniel,' said the niece calmly; 'he told me he had a horror of dogs. He was once hunted into a cemetery somewhere on the banks of the Ganges by a pack of pariah dogs, and had to spend the night in a newly dug grave with the creatures snarling and grinning and foaming just above him. Enough to make anyone lose their nerve.'

Romance at short notice was her speciality.

Did you realise all the time that Nuttel was being deceived, and that he was having a practical joke played on him? Or were you, too, taken in by the story? Did you distinguish between appearances

Fiction

and reality? Did your view of the open window change at the end of the story?

'Romance at short notice was her speciality' – a euphemism for 'she was a compulsive liar'. When it comes to creative writing, avoidance of 'plain English' can be an effective humorous effect.

> Framton grabbed wildly at his stick and hat; the hall door, the gravel drive, and the front gate were dimly noted stages in his headlong retreat.

This is a far more creative and humorous way of saying 'he ran away as fast as he could', and yet over-description is avoided. The image of him flailing up the drive is effectively represented in a short, succinct and funny way.

You can read the whole of this clever short story and some more classic works from Saki in the book *Beasts and Super-Beasts*, at: www.gutenberg.org/ebooks/269

Novels

A novel is an extended piece of fiction, usually with a number of different characters, a central plot that builds up to a climax and at least one sub-plot. There are many different types or genres of fiction. Here are just a few:

- mystery
- romance
- historical
- thriller
- science fiction

Although there are lots of different types of novels, there are certain elements that all novels have. These are as follows:

- **Setting**. The novel is always set in a certain time or place.
- **Plot**. This is the story that the novel is telling.
- **Narrator/voice**. This is the voice that's telling the story – it can be a first person narrator or third person narrator.
- **Dialogue**. This is the conversation that the characters have.
- **Characters**. These are the people in the story.
- **Theme**. This is the idea or message that runs throughout the story. Sometimes there can be more than one theme.

WRITING YOUR OWN FICTION COMPOSITION

We're now going to look at how you can apply these elements to your own compositions – whether you are writing a short story, a novella or a novel.

We are going to use a very famous novel to illustrate these characteristics. *Pride and Prejudice* was written by Jane Austen and published in 1813. It is one of the most popular novels ever written, and it has been adapted for film and TV. If you are studying English composition, it's a book you should read.

Jane Austen was born in 1775, and she wrote with insight, intelligence and wit about the social etiquette (the customs or rules controlling social and moral behaviour) of the upper classes of the period she lived in. Her main themes were how the upper classes interacted with each other, how they viewed love and the importance of marriage to a woman at that time. If you were angry in 19th-century English polite society, you couldn't show your feelings and shout. You had to be dignified at all times. If you were a woman and your parents couldn't provide for you and you didn't marry, you would either fall into dire poverty or have to become a dependent of another relative. Getting married – or getting daughters married – was therefore a big concern. *Pride and Prejudice* is set in this time, and deals with many of these themes, as well as how pride and prejudice can stop people from seeing things as they really are.

Setting

The setting is where the novel takes place. It can:

- create the atmosphere for your novel, and help your reader to imagine the scenes
- give information about a character – for example, if your character is a bit forgetful, you could show them rushing around the house looking for keys
- provide opportunities for a plot – for example, if your setting is in a major city and a meteor suddenly hits the Earth, then that's going to be interesting!

Jane Austen does all this brilliantly in her first chapter. We find out about Mr and Mrs Bennet and their five daughters, Mrs Bennet's obsession with getting her daughters married, and the sort of marriage that the couple themselves have. Austen

also sows the seeds of the plot, and tells us about contemporary social etiquette – or how you had to go about getting introduced to eligible young men.

It is a truth universally acknowledged, that a single man in possession of a good fortune, must be in want of a wife.

However little known the feelings or views of such a man may be on his first entering a neighbourhood, this truth is so well fixed in the minds of the surrounding families, that he is considered the rightful property of some one or other of their daughters.

'My dear Mr. Bennet,' said his lady to him one day, 'have you heard that Netherfield Park is let at last?'

Mr. Bennet replied that he had not.

'But it is,' returned she; 'for Mrs. Long has just been here, and she told me all about it.'

Mr. Bennet made no answer.

'Do you not want to know who has taken it?' cried his wife impatiently.

'You want to tell me, and I have no objection to hearing it.'

This was invitation enough.

'Why, my dear, you must know, Mrs. Long says that Netherfield is taken by a young man of large fortune from the north of England; that he came down

Setting

on Monday in a chaise and four to see the place, and was so much delighted with it, that he agreed with Mr. Morris immediately; that he is to take possession before Michaelmas, and some of his servants are to be in the house by the end of next week.'

'What is his name?'

'Bingley.'

'Is he married or single?'

'Oh! Single, my dear, to be sure! A single man of large fortune; four or five thousand a year. What a fine thing for our girls!'

'How so? How can it affect them?'

'My dear Mr. Bennet,' replied his wife, 'how can you be so tiresome! You must know that I am thinking of his marrying one of them.'

'Is that his design in settling here?'

'Design! Nonsense, how can you talk so! But it is very likely that he may fall in love with one of them, and therefore you must visit him as soon as he comes.'

'I see no occasion for that. You and the girls may go, or you may send them by themselves, which perhaps will be still better, for as you are as handsome as any of them, Mr. Bingley may like you the best of the party.'

'My dear, you flatter me. I certainly have had my share of beauty, but I do not pretend to be anything

Writing your own fiction composition

extraordinary now. When a woman has five grown-up daughters, she ought to give over thinking of her own beauty.'

'In such cases, a woman has not often much beauty to think of.'

'But, my dear, you must indeed go and see Mr. Bingley when he comes into the neighbourhood.'

'It is more than I engage for, I assure you.'

'But consider your daughters. Only think what an establishment it would be for one of them. Sir William and Lady Lucas are determined to go, merely on that account, for in general, you know, they visit no newcomers. Indeed you must go, for it will be impossible for us to visit him if you do not.'

'You are over-scrupulous, surely. I dare say Mr. Bingley will be very glad to see you; and I will send a few lines by you to assure him of my hearty consent to his marrying whichever he chooses of the girls; though I must throw in a good word for my little Lizzy.'

'I desire you will do no such thing. Lizzy is not a bit better than the others; and I am sure she is not half so handsome as Jane, nor half so good-humoured as Lydia. But you are always giving her the preference.'

'They have none of them much to recommend them,' replied he; 'they are all silly and ignorant like other girls;

but Lizzy has something more of quickness than her sisters.'

'Mr. Bennet, how can you abuse your own children in such a way? You take delight in vexing me. You have no compassion for my poor nerves.'

'You mistake me, my dear. I have a high respect for your nerves. They are my old friends. I have heard you mention them with consideration these last twenty years at least.'

'Ah, you do not know what I suffer.'

'But I hope you will get over it, and live to see many young men of four thousand a year come into the neighbourhood.'

'It will be no use to us, if twenty such should come, since you will not visit them.'

'Depend upon it, my dear, that when there are twenty, I will visit them all.'

Mr. Bennet was so odd a mixture of quick parts, sarcastic humour, reserve, and caprice, that the experience of three-and-twenty years had been insufficient to make his wife understand his character. Her mind was less difficult to develop. She was a woman of mean understanding, little information, and uncertain temper. When she was discontented, she fancied herself nervous. The business of her life was to get her daughters married; its solace was visiting and news.

Plot

Most novels tend to have the following plot outline or variations of this:

- **Exposition**. This is the early part of the novel, where we find out about the setting, characters and what the story is about.

- **Conflict**. This is usually introduced quite early on, and can be a conflict between two people, between people and nature or an internal conflict that somebody is having.

- **Rising action**. This is the stage of the novel where the conflict increases and the reader's sense of excitement, tension or interest increases accordingly.

- **Climax**. This marks the high point of the conflict, and usually means a turning point – either good or bad – for the main characters.

- **Falling action**. This follows the climax, when the reader's sense of excitement, tension or interest declines. This usually happens towards the end of the novel.

- **Resolution**. The character(s) deal with the conflict, and there is a natural ending to the story. This could be either good or bad.

Plot

Let's illustrate this by looking at the plot of *Pride and Prejudice*.

Exposition

We have already found out from the first chapter that Charles Bingley, a wealthy young gentleman has rented the manor of Netherfield Park. The Bennet household and the rest of the village of Longbourn are very excited about this news.

Mr and Mrs Bennet have five daughters called Jane, Elizabeth, Mary, Kitty and Lydia, and Mrs Bennet's main aim in life is to get them married to rich and respectable men. Mr Bennet pays a social visit to Mr Bingley, and the family attend a ball where Mr Bingley and his friend Mr Darcy are present.

Conflict

The conflict is introduced at the ball. Mr Bingley makes a good impression and is friendly with everybody, but his friend, Mr Darcy, appears to be haughty and unsociable, and – worst of all – he refuses to dance with Lizzy Bennet, which makes everybody think he is arrogant and rude:

Writing your own fiction composition

'Come, Darcy,' said he, 'I must have you dance. I hate to see you standing about by yourself in this stupid manner. You had much better dance.'

'I certainly shall not. You know how I detest it, unless I am particularly acquainted with my partner. At such an assembly as this it would be insupportable. Your sisters are engaged, and there is not another woman in the room whom it would not be a punishment to me to stand up with.'

'I would not be so fastidious as you are,' cried Mr. Bingley, 'for a kingdom! Upon my honour, I never met with so many pleasant girls in my life as I have this evening; and there are several of them you see uncommonly pretty.'

'You are dancing with the only handsome girl in the room,' said Mr. Darcy, looking at the eldest Miss Bennet.

'Oh! She is the most beautiful creature I ever beheld! But there is one of her sisters sitting down just behind you, who is very pretty, and I dare say very agreeable. Do let me ask my partner to introduce you.'

'Which do you mean?' and turning round he looked for a moment at Elizabeth, till catching her eye, he withdrew his own and coldly said:

'She is tolerable, but not handsome enough to tempt me; I am in no humour at present to give consequence

Plot

to young ladies who are slighted by other men. You had better return to your partner and enjoy her smiles, for you are wasting your time with me.'

Mr. Bingley followed his advice. Mr. Darcy walked off; and Elizabeth remained with no very cordial feelings toward him. She told the story, however, with great spirit among her friends; for she had a lively, playful disposition, which delighted in anything ridiculous.

Rising action

Jane and Bingley's relationship develops during a number of social events, and Jane is invited to visit Netherfield Park. She gets soaked on the way there and catches a cold. Elizabeth walks over to Netherfield to make sure her sister is well, and arrives looking mud-spattered and windswept. Mr Bingley's sister makes sarcastic remarks about her, and tries to get Darcy to agree with her. However, Elizabeth and Darcy have been thrown together at a number of social functions since the ball, and he has become increasingly attracted to her.

Occupied in observing Mr. Bingley's attentions to her sister, Elizabeth was far from suspecting that she was herself becoming an object of some interest in

Writing your own fiction composition

the eyes of his friend. Mr. Darcy had at first scarcely allowed her to be pretty; he had looked at her without admiration at the ball; and when they next met, he looked at her only to criticise. But no sooner had he made it clear to himself and his friends that she hardly had a good feature in her face, than he began to find it was rendered uncommonly intelligent by the beautiful expression of her dark eyes. To this discovery succeeded some others equally mortifying. Though he had detected with a critical eye more than one failure of perfect symmetry in her form, he was forced to acknowledge her figure to be light and pleasing; and in spite of his asserting that her manners were not those of the fashionable world, he was caught by their easy playfulness. Of this she was perfectly unaware; to her he was only the man who made himself agreeable nowhere, and who had not thought her handsome enough to dance with.

Mr Bingley's sisters, however, think that Jane and Elizabeth are beneath them socially, and don't try to hide their scorn:

'I have an excessive regard for Miss Jane Bennet, she is really a very sweet girl, and I wish with all my heart she were well settled. But with such a father and mother, and such low connections, I am afraid there is no chance of it.'

'I think I have heard you say that their uncle is an attorney in Meryton.'

'Yes; and they have another, who lives somewhere near Cheapside.'

'That is capital,' added her sister, and they both laughed heartily.

'If they had uncles enough to fill all Cheapside,' cried Bingley, 'it would not make them one jot less agreeable.'

'But it must very materially lessen their chance of marrying men of any consideration in the world,' replied Darcy.

To this speech Bingley made no answer; but his sisters gave it their hearty assent, and indulged their mirth for some time at the expense of their dear friend's vulgar relations.

Jane and Elizabeth return home to find that Mr Collins is visiting. Mr Collins is a clergyman who will inherit Mr Bennet's property when he dies, because the girls can't inherit the property and he is the nearest male heir. Mr Collins is pompous and arrogant. He proposes to Elizabeth, who refuses him. He is very offended. Meanwhile, some militia officers have been stationed near Longbourn, and are introduced to the Bennet girls. One of them, Wickham, is a handsome soldier whom Elizabeth finds attractive. He tells her that Darcy has cheated him out of his inheritance. Because of how Darcy treated her, Elizabeth is ready to believe him.

At the beginning of winter, there are two unexpected events: the Bingleys and Darcy suddenly leave Netherfield for London, leaving Jane upset and disappointed, and Mr Collins announces that he has become engaged to Charlotte Lucas, Elizabeth's best friend, and the poor daughter of a local knight. Elizabeth is shocked at this, but Charlotte explains that her parents can't support her, and she needs to get married for financial reasons. Elizabeth promises to visit them. Jane, meanwhile, visits London, hoping that she might see Bingley. While she is there, Miss Bingley visits her and is rude to her, and Bingley doesn't visit at all.

This is the worst point of Elizabeth and Jane's fortunes. However, the tension and excitement build up again when Elizabeth visits Charlotte

Plot

and Mr Collins. They live near Lady Catherine de Bourgh, who is Darcy's aunt. Elizabeth and Darcy are thrown together socially several times, and we are aware of Darcy's increasing attraction to Elizabeth. However, Colonel Fitzwilliam, Darcy's friend and cousin who is also visiting Lady Catherine, unwittingly tells Elizabeth that it was Darcy who persuaded Bingley not to marry Jane. Elizabeth is devastated.

Climax

When the climax comes, it is unexpected and very dramatic. Darcy visits Elizabeth at the Collins' home and completely shocks her by telling her that he loves her (despite the fact that he has fought against it):

'In vain I have struggled. It will not do. My feelings will not be repressed. You must allow me to tell you how ardently I admire and love you.'

Elizabeth's astonishment was beyond expression. She stared, coloured, doubted, and was silent. This he considered sufficient encouragement; and the avowal of all that he felt, and had long felt for her, immediately followed. He spoke well; but there were feelings besides

Writing your own fiction composition

those of the heart to be detailed; and he was not more eloquent on the subject of tenderness than of pride. His sense of her inferiority – of its being a degradation – of the family obstacles which had always opposed to inclination, were dwelt on with a warmth which seemed due to the consequence he was wounding, but was very unlikely to recommend his suit.

Elizabeth tells Darcy that he is arrogant and accuses him of persuading Bingley not to marry Jane, and of disinheriting Wickham. She refuses him:

'From the very beginning – from the first moment, I may almost say – of my acquaintance with you, your manners, impressing me with the fullest belief of your arrogance, your conceit, and your selfish disdain of the feelings of others, were such as to form the groundwork of disapprobation on which succeeding events have built so immovable a dislike; and I had not known you a month before I felt that you were the last man in the world whom I could ever be prevailed on to marry.'

He replies, very formally:

Plot

'You have said quite enough, madam. I perfectly comprehend your feelings, and have now only to be ashamed of what my own have been. Forgive me for having taken up so much of your time, and accept my best wishes for your health and happiness.'

This is a great example of verbal sword-play with manners.

Darcy leaves but returns with a letter, and it is this that is the climax of the conflict, and the turning point for Elizabeth. In the letter Darcy admits that he persuaded Bingley to distance himself from Jane, but this was because he didn't think that Jane cared much for his friend. He also says that the reason he fell out with Wickham was because Wickham tried to elope with his young sister, Georgiana, to inherit her money.

The letter makes Elizabeth see Darcy in a different light – she starts to lose her prejudice against him.

Falling action

This process continues when she returns home. The militia (with Wickham) is leaving town, and

Writing your own fiction composition

Lydia persuades her father to give her permission to stay with an old colonel in Brighton, where Wickham's regiment is to be stationed. Elizabeth begs him to refuse Lydia permission, but he gives in.

Elizabeth then goes on a trip to Derbyshire with her aunt and uncle, the Gardiners. They visit Pemberley, Darcy's estate, believing that Darcy is away. Darcy's servants obviously love him, and say that he is a wonderful master. Darcy arrives unexpectedly, but behaves warmly and kindly to Elizabeth and the Gardiners, and invites them to be his guests. They meet his sister, Georgiana. Elizabeth realises that her feelings towards him are changing:

As for Elizabeth, her thoughts were at Pemberley this evening more than the last; and the evening, though as it passed it seemed long, was not long enough to determine her feelings towards one in that mansion; and she lay awake two whole hours endeavouring to make them out. She certainly did not hate him. No; hatred had vanished long ago, and she had almost as long been ashamed of ever feeling a dislike against him, that could be so called. The respect created by the conviction of his valuable qualities, though at first unwillingly admitted, had for some time ceased to be repugnant to her feeling; and it was now heightened into somewhat of a friendlier nature, by the testimony so highly in his favour, and bringing forward his disposition in so amiable a light, which yesterday had produced. But above all, above respect and esteem, there was a motive within her of goodwill which could not be overlooked.

It was gratitude; gratitude, not merely for having once loved her, but for loving her still well enough to forgive all the petulance and acrimony of her manner in rejecting him, and all the unjust accusations accompanying her rejection. He who, she had been persuaded, would avoid her as his greatest enemy, seemed, on this accidental meeting, most eager to preserve the acquaintance, and without any indelicate display of regard, or any peculiarity of manner, where their two selves only were concerned, was soliciting the good opinion of her friends, and bent on making her known to his sister. Such a change in a man of so much pride exciting not only astonishment but gratitude – for to love, ardent love, it must be attributed; and as such its impression on her was of a sort to be encouraged, as by no means unpleasing, though it could not be exactly defined. She respected, she esteemed, she was grateful to him, she felt a real interest in his welfare;

Writing your own fiction composition

and she only wanted to know how far she wished that welfare to depend upon herself, and how far it would be for the happiness of both that she should employ the power, which her fancy told her she still possessed, of bringing on her the renewal of his addresses.

But then comes a bombshell – Elizabeth receives a letter from Jane saying that Lydia has run off with Wickham, and that nobody can find them. If they are living together and aren't married, the whole family will be disgraced. Elizabeth goes home, and a letter eventually comes from Mr Gardiner saying that the couple have been found, and that Wickham has agreed to marry Lydia in exchange for an annual income. Lydia and Wickham return briefly to Longbourn as a married couple, and Lydia lets it slip that Darcy paid Wickham off and saved the family's reputation.

Resolution

By this point, we are desperate for a happy-ever-after resolution – especially after all those trials and tribulations. And this is exactly what Jane Austen signposts in the falling action and delivers to us in the resolution. It all works out beautifully in the end. Bingley returns to Netherfield and proposes to Jane. That same night Lady Catherine visits Elizabeth and says she has heard that Darcy is planning to marry her. She tries to bully Elizabeth into promising that she won't marry him because she is so far beneath him on the social scale, but Elizabeth refuses. As she says:

> 'I am only resolved to act in that manner, which will, in my own opinion, constitute my happiness, without reference to you, or to any person so wholly unconnected with me.'

Darcy obviously hears about this exchange and it makes him think that Elizabeth's feelings towards him could have changed. Several days later, he visits the Bennets with Bingley and goes for a walk with Elizabeth. During the walk, he proposes and tells her that he knew she would have told his aunt if she definitely didn't want to marry him:

> 'It taught me to hope,' said he, 'as I had scarcely ever allowed myself to hope before. I knew enough of your disposition to be certain that, had you been absolutely,

Writing your own fiction composition

irrevocably decided against me, you would have acknowledged it to Lady Catherine, frankly and openly.'

So there was a double wedding with Jane, Bingley, Elizabeth and Darcy, and they all lived happily ever after.

Narrator/voice

The narrator is the voice that is telling the story. It can either be in the first person, where someone is talking to the reader directly – for example, 'I did this' and 'I said' – or in the third person, where 'he', 'she' or 'they' tell the story, and it's up to the reader to form a view of the characters.

The narrator or voice in *Pride and Prejudice* is in the third person omniscient – this means that the narrator knows and describes the thoughts and feelings of all the people in the story. But the narrator tells the story through Elizabeth's eyes and from her point of view. She is in every chapter and in the pivotal Chapter 36 (the climax of the book after she has read Darcy's letter) the narrator tells us about the emotional transformation she goes through as a result. The narrator tells us what people say and do, how they behave and what they think through the use of dialogue. Sometimes the narrator is very judgemental, but very funny. Here's an example:

Mr. Collins was not a sensible man, and the deficiency of nature had been but little assisted by education or society; the greatest part of his life having been spent under the guidance of an illiterate and miserly father; and though he belonged to one of the universities, he had merely kept the necessary terms, without forming at it any useful acquaintance. The subjection in which his father had brought him up had given him originally great humility of manner; but it was now a good deal counteracted by the self-conceit of a weak head, living in retirement, and the consequential feelings of early and unexpected prosperity. A fortunate chance had recommended him to Lady Catherine de Bourgh when the living of Hunsford was vacant; and the respect which he felt for her high rank, and his veneration for her as his patroness, mingling with a very good opinion of himself, of his authority as a clergyman, and his right as a rector, made him altogether a mixture of pride and obsequiousness, self-importance and humility.

Writing your own fiction composition

Dialogue

The dialogue is the conversations that the characters have. The dialogue spoken in *Pride and Prejudice* is extremely witty and well-observed, and it is the main way that Jane Austen tells us about her characters. For example, Mrs Bennet and Lydia, her favourite, come across as being silly, shallow women. Lydia has nearly plunged the family into complete disgrace, but she has absolutely no remorse or insight into what she has done – and neither does her mother. Her main concern is that she got married first before her sisters, and she boasts about being able to find husbands for them:

'Well, mamma,' said she, when they were all returned to the breakfast room, 'and what do you think of my husband? Is not he a charming man? I am sure my sisters must all envy me. I only hope they may have half my good luck. They must all go to Brighton. That is the place to get husbands. What a pity it is, mamma, we did not all go.'

'Very true; and if I had my will, we should. But my dear Lydia, I don't at all like your going such a way off. Must it be so?'

'Oh, lord! yes;—there is nothing in that. I shall like

Characters

it of all things. You and papa, and my sisters, must come down and see us. We shall be at Newcastle all the winter, and I dare say there will be some balls, and I will take care to get good partners for them all.'

'I should like it beyond anything!' said her mother.

'And then when you go away, you may leave one or two of my sisters behind you; and I dare say I shall get husbands for them before the winter is over.'

Characters

Characters are the imaginary people that you write about in your book or composition. If your characters aren't interesting and realistic, they won't work. They also need to be contrasting to provide drama and conflict in the plot.

For example, the characters in *Pride and Prejudice* range from stupid and shallow, to witty and intelligent, to deceitful. They are complicated and fascinating and hook the reader into the story. Let's look at the main characters in the novel, and what they are like.

Elizabeth

Elizabeth is the heroine of the novel. She is her father's favourite, and is witty, intelligent and attractive, with a 'fine pair of eyes'. She stands up for herself against Lady Catherine, although Catherine is far above her in social standing. She is loyal and loving. She walks three miles to take care of her sister. However, she allows herself to be prejudiced against Darcy, and this prevents her from seeing through Wickham.

Darcy

Darcy is the hero of the novel. He is from a very old and reputable family. He is proud, and he can act in a superior and arrogant way, as if he is better than everybody else. This isn't always intentional – it's because he is shy and reserved. He is very kind and generous to those he loves and cares about (family, friends and servants). He pays off Wickham. He becomes very attracted to Elizabeth, but has to fight his pride and prejudices to admit that and propose to her.

Jane

Jane is the oldest and most beautiful of the Bennet girls. She is a very good person, and can never see the bad in anybody. She and Elizabeth are very close and support each other. She can be quiet and

Characters

reserved, and Darcy misinterprets this as lack of interest.

Bingley
Bingley's money comes from his father's business – it isn't inherited like Darcy's. Bingley's personality is like Jane's – he is very easy going and charming. He isn't bothered about Jane's social standing, but he does allow Darcy to persuade him to leave her, so he doesn't seem to be very strong minded.

Wickham
Wickham is a smooth-talking liar, who spends the money Darcy gives him and then tries to get more by eloping with his sister, Georgiana. When that doesn't succeed, he elopes with Lydia Bennet, who is only sixteen. He is the opposite of Darcy, but Elizabeth is still duped by him because of her prejudice against Darcy.

Mrs Bennet
Mrs Bennet's only interest in life is getting her daughters married off. She doesn't really care about the true happiness of her daughters – only

how things look – hence her reaction to Lydia's marriage to Wickham. She is shallow, lacking in sensitivity and acts inappropriately, to the embarrassment of her family – particularly Elizabeth and Jane.

Mr Bennet

Mr Bennet married the wrong person, and is now having to put up with it. He is intelligent, witty and loves reading, and goes to his library to get peace and quiet. He and Elizabeth get on very well. He wants a quiet life and isn't strict enough when he needs to be (for example, when he lets Lydia go to Brighton). He can make insensitive comments, but he loves his daughters and wants what is best for them.

Mr Collins

Mr Collins is a bit of a comic character. He is a clergyman, but doesn't act like one. He is pompous rather than humble, although he pretends to be. He doesn't appear to have genuine feelings, because he was able to propose to Jane, Elizabeth and then Charlotte in quick succession. His speech and manner are overly formal and verging on the ridiculous, and he is obsessed with Lady Catherine's favour.

Lady Catherine de Bourgh

Lady Catherine is at the top of the social ladder, and she knows it. She is a bit of a caricature of the worst characteristics of the upper classes. She's a bully who is rude and insensitive and expects people to do what she wants without question. She hates Elizabeth because she stands up to her. Unlike Darcy, Lady Catherine has no manners.

Themes

A theme is an idea that runs throughout the story. There can be more than one theme in a novel. Themes give a novel more depth – they make it about more than just a story – there are hidden meanings lying underneath.

The themes in *Pride and Prejudice* include:

- pride and prejudice (obviously)
- love and marriage
- reputation
- class and social standing

Writing your own fiction composition

Pride

Pride is having too high an opinion of your worth or importance. Prejudice is making judgements about other people without really knowing them or knowing the facts about them. There are examples of how pride and prejudice affect characters' behaviour and actions all through the novel.

For example, Mr Darcy appears to be very proud of his social standing, and gives a bad impression to strangers:

… but his friend Mr. Darcy soon drew the attention of the room by his fine, tall person, handsome features, noble mien, and the report which was in general circulation within five minutes after his entrance, of his having ten thousand a year. The gentlemen pronounced him to be a fine figure of a man, the ladies declared he was much handsomer than Mr. Bingley, and he was looked at with great admiration for about half the evening, till his manners gave a disgust which turned the tide of his popularity; for he was discovered to be proud; to be above his company, and above being pleased; and not all his large estate in Derbyshire could then save him from having a most forbidding, disagreeable countenance, and being unworthy to be compared with his friend.

Themes

Lady Catherine on the other hand is deliberately proud – she is at the top of the social ladder, and she wants to make sure that everybody knows it.

When the ladies returned to the drawing-room, there was little to be done but to hear Lady Catherine talk, which she did without any intermission till coffee came in, delivering her opinion on every subject in so decisive a manner, as proved that she was not used to have her judgement controverted. She inquired into Charlotte's domestic concerns familiarly and minutely, gave her a great deal of advice as to the management of them all; told her how everything ought to be regulated in so small a family as hers, and instructed her as to the care of her cows and her poultry. Elizabeth found that nothing was beneath this great lady's attention, which could furnish her with an occasion of dictating to others.

Prejudice

Darcy forms a prejudice against the Bennets, without really knowing them.

Elizabeth isn't normally prejudiced, but Darcy's refusal to dance with her offends her and hurts her pride. This leads her to develop a prejudice against him, and she makes everything about him from this point on fit this prejudice – that's why she is willing to believe Wickham.

Mrs Bennet's prejudice against Darcy becomes downright open and embarrassing – although she seems to forget it right away when he proposes to Elizabeth.

'Good gracious! Lord bless me! only think! dear me! Mr. Darcy! Who would have thought it! And is it really true? Oh! my sweetest Lizzy! how rich and how great you will be! What pin-money, what jewels, what carriages you will have! Jane's is nothing to it—nothing at all. I am so pleased—so happy. Such a charming man!—so handsome! so tall!—Oh, my dear Lizzy! pray apologise for my having disliked him so much before. I hope he will overlook it. Dear, dear Lizzy. A house in town! Every thing that is charming! Three daughters married! Ten thousand a year! Oh, Lord! What will become of me. I shall go distracted.'

This was enough to prove that her approbation need not be doubted: and Elizabeth, rejoicing that such an effusion was heard only by herself, soon went away. But before she had been three minutes in her own room, her mother followed her.

'My dearest child,' she cried, 'I can think of nothing

Themes

else! Ten thousand a year, and very likely more! 'Tis as good as a Lord! And a special licence. You must and shall be married by a special licence. But my dearest love, tell me what dish Mr. Darcy is particularly fond of, that I may have it to-morrow.'

Love and marriage

The different types of love and marriage are another main theme of the book. For most women in the nineteenth century (unless they were very rich and financially independent), marriage was essential for their financial security and social standing. Charlotte Lucas is a good example of this – her parents are too poor to support her, so she has to jump at the first chance of a decent match. Otherwise, she will be left in poverty, or will have to rely on the charity of friends or relatives – not a good position to be in. She is willing to marry Mr Collins and put up with him for the financial security, social standing and reputation he will bring her:

'I see what you are feeling,' replied Charlotte. 'You must be surprised, very much surprised – so lately as Mr. Collins was wishing to marry you. But when you have had time to think it over, I hope you will be satisfied with what I have done. I am not romantic, you know; I never was. I ask only a comfortable home; and considering Mr. Collins's character, connection, and situation in life, I am convinced that my chance of happiness with him is as fair as most people can boast on entering the marriage state.'

Mr Bennet married Mrs Bennet because she was beautiful – but regretted it very quickly afterwards because she is shallow and embarrassing and they have nothing in common. He now avoids her by spending a lot of time in the library. Elizabeth can see this relationship, and doesn't want it herself.

Darcy and Elizabeth have it all – they have overcome obstacles, learned about themselves and each other and have a mutual love and respect for each other's qualities.

Reputation

Reputation in Jane Austen's time was everything. If a member of the family lost their reputation, the rest of the family was disgraced – and that meant being outcast from 'good society'. This is why Elizabeth is devastated when she hears about

A good beginning and a good end

Lydia eloping with Wickham – if they aren't married, it will bring disgrace on all the family, and nobody will marry any of the girls because they will be tainted with it. Lydia seems blissfully ignorant of or insensitive to this.

Class and social standing

Again, social standing was key in Austen's day – who you were and where you were on the social ladder and what people thought of you were of great importance. Elizabeth isn't as concerned as other people about reputation – she is prepared to stand up to Lady Catherine and walk to Netherfield and get muddy because she doesn't care very much what people think.

Mrs Bennet, on the other hand, is more concerned that Lydia has gotten a husband than she is about the fact that she has married a selfish, lazy liar.

A good beginning and a good end

It's important in any piece of fiction writing to have a good beginning and a good end.

A good beginning will get the reader hooked, and a good ending should provide a resolution to the story. The reader should feel that this resolution was inevitable.

The first chapter of *Pride and Prejudice* hooks the reader in immediately, and sets the tone for the whole novel with one of the most famous and witty lines in English literature:

> It is a truth universally acknowledged, that a single man in possession of a good fortune, must be in want of a wife.

We know because of the various signposts in the climax and falling action that there is going to be a happy ending – although Austen throws in the news about Lydia and Wickham to create tension and worry us for a few pages. Everything is resolved as it should be in the ending, and we are left feeling that really, it couldn't have ended any other way.

The writing process – fiction

We have looked at all the different elements that you need to think about in fiction writing and have illustrated these with examples. Now we're going to look at the actual writing process that every writer goes through. Understanding this process

The writing process – fiction

should help you when you write your own compositions. This process doesn't have to be linear, where each stage is only done once. You can repeat different parts of the process and revise your work until you are happy with it.

Here's an example of a process you could use:

- **What is the story you want to tell?** What is your story about? Is it a real-life story or one that you have created yourself? Once you know this, you can work on the plot, characters, dialogue and setting.

- **Brainstorm your ideas**. People can find it very stressful if they are faced with a blank piece of paper. Don't panic. Instead, write down all your ideas about the story/plot, your setting, characters and dialogue. What is the narrative voice – first person or third person? What sort of structure are you going to use? Are you going to tell the story from start to finish, or use flashbacks, or put it in the form of a diary?

- **Plan and develop your structure**. Write down notes under chapter headings – where does the story get to during each chapter? What is the conflict and when is it introduced? What is the climax in the story and when is it introduced? What is the resolution? How is your story going to end? Having the big picture of your story before you write it can make it easier to follow the plot and not get lost. Apparently JK Rowling, author of the Harry Potter books, wrote out the entire plot of all seven books during a long train journey.

- **Write the first draft.** Don't worry too much at this stage about getting everything perfect – you can come back to it and edit it later.

- **Revise and edit your work.** Read over your story objectively. Does the plot make sense? Does it flow? Does the dialogue sound realistic? Are the characters believable? Ask a 'critical friend' to read it over and give you their honest feedback.

- **Cut out anything you don't need.** Editing also reveals repetition and unnecessary detail.

- **Write the final draft.**

If you don't have a complete story in mind, though, this doesn't mean you can't start writing.

If you are having problems getting initial ideas, there are plenty of things you can do to spark inspiration. Don't let yourself be intimidated by an empty page: write ideas, character sketches and dialogue without worrying about where it's going to go. Once you have a story in mind which catches your imagination you can then follow the kind of process above.

Writing exercises and prompts can be useful for coming up with ideas or just as a warm-up exercise, to get you over initial hesitancy and into the right mind-frame to write. There are many books of these available, as well as websites, including blogs which post new prompts regularly and often allow you to post your own work in reply.

Try some of the following sites:

www.creativewritingprompts.com
www.writersdigest.com/prompts
storyaday.org/category/inspiration/writing-prompts/
andrewbosley.weebly.com/the-brainstormer.html

You could also try a plot generator, which sets you a scenario to work from in your story, as here:

www.archetypewriting.com/muse/generators/plot.html

Writing your own fiction composition

First lines

Starting any work of fiction can be intimidating: the pressure to get the 'perfect' first line can leave you staring at a blank page, unable to get to the story itself. A good way to deal with this, as well as to spark first ideas, is to write first lines for stories – as many as possible. You don't need to do anything further with these if you don't wish to, or have any idea of what the story itself would be about. If you feel inspired to continue on with a story you have started in this way, great. If not, writing lots of first lines will still help in getting over the stumbling block you may experience between having an idea and putting pen to paper – as well as teaching you to recognise a good first line.

So what makes a good first line? Here are some famous examples to consider:

> And after all the weather was ideal.
> *The Garden Party*, Katherine Mansfield

> A green and yellow parrot, which hung in a cage outside the door, kept repeating over and over:
> 'Allez vous-en! Allez vous-en! Sapristi! That's all right!'
> *The Awakening*, Kate Chopin

The writing process – fiction

I first heard of Ántonia on what seemed to me an interminable journey across the great midland plain of North America.

My Ántonia, Willa Cather

While the present century was in its teens, and on one sunshiny morning in June, there drove up to the great iron gate of Miss Pinkerton's academy for young ladies, on Chiswick Mall, a large family coach, with two fat horses in blazing harness, driven by a fat coachman in a three-cornered hat and wig, at the rate of four miles an hour.

Vanity Fair, William Makepeace Thackeray

There was no hope for him this time: it was the third stroke.

Dubliners, James Joyce

1801. – I have just returned from a visit to my landlord – the solitary neighbour that I shall be troubled with.

Wuthering Heights, Emily Brontë

Happy families are all alike; every unhappy family is unhappy in its own way.

Anna Karenina, Leo Tolstoy

Writing your own fiction composition

I had the story, bit by bit, from various people, and, as generally happens in such cases, each time it was a different story.

Ethan Frome, Edith Wharton

Mr. Sherlock Holmes, who was usually very late in the mornings, save upon those not infrequent occasions when he was up all night, was seated at the breakfast table.

The Hound of the Baskervilles, Sir Arthur Conan Doyle

These openings are all vastly different in what they tell us about the story to follow. Some establish the point of view of the story (first person or third person), or its form (diary entries in Brontë's case). Some establish setting. Some introduce the protagonist or a major character. (Conan Doyle even introduces some of his character and habits.)

Wharton and Cather both introduce the idea of a narrator reminiscing, looking back on completed or past events. Tolstoy and Wharton both start with a generalisation or a universal truth. Thackeray gives us a more traditional sense of a narrator beginning to tell us a story, while Mansfield gives

The writing process – fiction

us the sense that we've barged in upon our narrator mid-thought.

Joyce tells us very little about the story to follow, merely suggesting a sense of mood – of foreboding – while Thackeray throws in the metaphorical kitchen sink with the amount of information provided. (Thackeray here illustrates the fact that rules are made to be broken: for all that authors would usually be told not to bombard the reader with too much detail right at the beginning, here he does exactly the opposite, to great comic effect.)

So what, if anything, do they have in common? They all, in their diverse ways, hook the reader into the story – grab our attention with a character, with a thought, with dialogue or an engaging image (both in the case of Chopin's talking parrot), with a vividly introduced setting or mood, or with the direct appeal of a first-person narrator. They all throw us right into things rather than losing our attention with introductory build-up before the story begins. Even Thackeray's sentence, with its more traditional format where the narrative voice is consciously introducing us to a story, puts us straight into the events of the novel, with the action of the coach drawing up on the morning described. This is beginning *in medias res* (in the middle of things) and is key to grabbing your reader's attention.

Now try writing ten of your own opening sentences.

Setting the scene

This time, let's look at some examples of writers introducing setting:

> The studio was filled with the rich odour of roses, and when the light summer wind stirred amidst the trees of the garden, there came through the open door the heavy scent of the lilac, or the more delicate perfume of the pink-flowering thorn.
>
> *The Picture of Dorian Gray*, Oscar Wilde

> The particular Jelly-bean patch which produced the protagonist of this history lies somewhere between the two—a little city of forty thousand that has dozed sleepily for forty thousand years in southern Georgia, occasionally stirring in its slumbers and muttering something about a war that took place sometime, somewhere, and that everyone else has forgotten long ago.
>
> *The Jelly-Bean*, F Scott Fitzgerald

The writing process – fiction

Wuthering Heights is the name of Mr. Heathcliff's dwelling. 'Wuthering' being a significant provincial adjective, descriptive of the atmospheric tumult to which its station is exposed in stormy weather. Pure, bracing ventilation they must have up there at all times, indeed: one may guess the power of the north wind blowing over the edge, by the excessive slant of a few stunted firs at the end of the house; and by a range of gaunt thorns all stretching their limbs one way, as if craving alms of the sun. Happily, the architect had foresight to build it strong: the narrow windows are deeply set in the wall, and the corners defended with large jutting stones.

Wuthering Heights, Emily Brontë

Take a mining townlet like Woodhouse, with a population of ten thousand people, and three generations behind it. This space of three generations argues a certain well-established society. The old 'County' has fled from the sight of so much disembowelled coal, to flourish on mineral rights in regions still idyllic. Remains one great and inaccessible magnate, the local coal owner: three generations old, and clambering on the bottom step of the 'County', kicking off the mass below. Rule him out.

The Lost Girl, DH Lawrence

These examples again show the diverse options open to writers. Some introduce the physical setting, relying on the senses, while some introduce the personality or structure of the society described. All create a mood which informs how we picture the setting described (compare the sensual tranquillity of Wilde's studio to the aged backwardness of Fitzgerald's Jelly-bean patch; the barren desolation of Brontë's tortured landscape and precarious house to the anxious, unsettled society suggested in Lawrence's townlet).

Use one (or all) of these four examples as your inspiration to introduce a setting of your own. Write a description of a setting dominated by a sense other than sight (as Wilde does); use personification (describing it as if it were a person) to introduce a setting's personality (as Fitzgerald does); use the eyes of a character who is a newcomer, seeing the place, as we are, for the first time (as Brontë does); or speak directly to your reader to create an unusual hook (as Lawrence does).

Prompts

Some of the books and websites mentioned above use prompts, rather than the kinds of exercises we have just done, as writers' tools. These can be small snippets (a photograph, a line of poetry, a quote, a theme) that you can use as inspiration to write your own piece – a kind of mental stepping stone. They can also be short story summaries which contain more detail (the plot outline, a character or event to be included, other themes). It is remarkable just how vastly different writers' finished pieces can be which use the same line or event as a leaping-off point. Using this kind of prompt helps you to focus on one thing in order to begin writing, but it doesn't limit creativity. The possibilities for your unique creation are still endless.

NON-FICTION

Non-fiction covers a very wide range, from biographies to scientific and technical writing to dictionaries.

In this section, we are going to examine some of the different types of non-fiction writing – including biographies, travel, cookery, technical and reference materials – and what they involve.

Non-fiction

We will then look at some of the things you need to think about when you are composing your own non-fiction writing.

Biographies

A biography presents the facts about the subject's life. (The subject is the person who is being written about. He or she is or was usually famous for some reason.) It usually interprets these facts to explain and help the reader to understand the individual's feelings and motivations, and the effect they have had on local, national or international events or on history.

Biographies tend to have the following characteristics:

- start with birth or early life and covers birth to present day or death
- look at the subject's formative years to understand and explore early influences on their later life
- put the subject's life in a historical and/or cultural context
- use direct quotes from the subject and those who knew them

Biographies

- use pictures, maps, photographs or other documents
- reflect the biographer's point of view, agenda or purpose in reporting the subject's life
- involve a lot of research including the person's actions and words, interviews with friends, relatives and critics, and secondary sources such as books, magazines and journals.

Bookshelves, libraries and websites are full of biographies about famous people from every walk of life such as politicians, actors, royalty, explorers, writers, artists, scientists, and so on.

Examples from two different biographies

You might want to write a short biography about a colleague or somebody who is taking part in your amateur dramatic society, for example. The same principles apply to each. You will need to carry out research using interviews as well as primary and secondary sources.

Here is an example of the opening section of a biography about James Joyce, author of *Ulysses*, by David Pritchard.

Non-fiction

James Joyce was not a man to underestimate his own importance, and if asked what great event took place in 1882 he might well have replied that he was born in that year. Yet 1882 was notable in Irish history for a number of other reasons. Politically speaking its most consequential event was the signing of the 'Kilmainham Treaty' between Charles Stewart Parnell, leader of the Irish Home Rule Party, and the English Prime Minister William Ewart Gladstone. The deal resulted in a series of land reforms that changed the face of rural Ireland and in time broke up the great estates of the Anglo-Irish ascendancy. Political unrest in Ireland that year resulted in two notable terrorist attacks – the Phoenix Park murders of Lord Lieutenant Cavendish and Secretary Burke, and the Maamtrasna massacre of a family of five peasants on the present borders of Counties Mayo and Galway. The second crime was followed by the conviction and hanging of three men, and the imprisonment of several others. By the purest of coincidences most of those involved in the mass murder – victims, perpetrators and witnesses – bore the surname Joyce.

Extract taken from *James Joyce*, by David Pritchard (Geddes & Grosset, 2001)

Biographies

The biographer, David Pritchard, immediately puts Joyce's birth in a historical context, grounding his subject within the story of his native land. By linking Joyce's birth with these momentous historical events, Pritchard establishes from the off his subject's identity as an Irish author, as well as giving us an indirect sense of the author's birth being a momentous event in itself. In his comment on Joyce's perspective on this, Pritchard also gives us an immediate sense of his subject's personality. The close of this first paragraph, while fortuitous, is used to neatly link the historical events described to the book's subject, bringing us back in to focus specifically on Joyce.

Quotes from letters and interviews, with the subject and with those who knew them, secondary sources, documents and photographs all help to make a biography engaging and authoritative. The amount of research and time that goes into writing any such biography of a major figure is considerable, but even if you won't ever have to write anything that long, reading these biographies, and analysing the techniques their authors have used, is of huge use for any biography writing you may do.

Non-fiction

Here is another example, from a biography of Robert Burns, the famous 18th-century Scottish poet who wrote 'To a Mouse'.

This extract describes early influences on the poet's life, and uses a direct quote from one of his letters to describe the effect of his first romance.

Before he was sixteen years old, Robert had worked his way through a large and very varied amount of literature. John Murdoch's teaching and Robert's own aptitude had made him an excellent English scholar. Wherever he went he carried with him a book of songs:

'I pored over them, driving my cart or walking to labour, song by song, verse by verse, carefully noting the true, tender or sublime from affectation and fustian.'

At the age of fifteen, Robert Burns 'committed the sin of Rhyme' – he fell in love and wrote his first song, 'Handsome Nell' [*see* page 209]:

O once I lov'd a bonnie lass,
An aye I love her still,
An' whilst that virtue warms my breast
I'll love my handsome Nell.

Biographies

Robert wrote:

'You know your country custom of coupling a man and woman together as partners in the labours of Harvest. In my fifteenth autumn my partner was a bewitching creature who just counted an autumn less. My scarcity of English denies me the power of doing her justice in that language, but you know the Scotch idiom. She was a bonnie, sweet, sonsie lass. In short, she altogether unwittingly to herself, initiated me in a certain delicious Passion, which in spite of acid Disappointment, gin-horse Prudence, and bookworm Philosophy, I hold to be the first of human joys, our dearest pleasure here below . . . I did not know well myself, why I liked so much to loiter behind with her, when returning in the evening from our labours; why the tones of her voice made my heartstrings thrill like an Eolian harp; and particularly, why my pulse beat such a furious ratann when I looked and fingered over her hand, to pick out the nettle-stings and thistles . . . Thus with me began Love and Poesy.'

Extract taken from *Robert Burns in Your Pocket*, pp.15–17 (Waverley Books, 2009)

Non-fiction

Travel

There are two main types of travel writing – travel articles and travel guides.

Travel articles

Travel articles give the reader a clear, strong impression of a place. As a travel writer, your role is to report on the main features of a destination, provide essential information for travellers, but also to give your unique slant on the sights, sounds and experiences they will have there.

Travel writers use many different styles and techniques, but the best travel articles usually have the following characteristics:

- good, practical information that is useful to the reader
- use of the writer's personal experiences, anecdotes and quotations to bring the article to life
- strong sense of the writer's personality – this gives the article a unique style
- a 'show, not tell' approach to the places, people and things they are writing about – showing creates a mental picture for the reader, and this makes them more engaged with the article

Travel

- a clear, concise writing style (in plain English)
- a central theme – the 'big picture' – that the writer works their impressions and facts around, and that acts as a structure for the piece.

Examples of a travel article

Now let's look at an example of a travel article, by journalist Garry Fraser in *The Scots Magazine*. It describes a trip around Lanarkshire, in the central lowlands of Scotland. It was historically closely linked with the coal industry, and has attractions today which bear witness to this part of its past.

When you read this extract, think about how the writer uses his experiences and anecdotes to bring the article to life. His writing is clear and concise, with touches of humour, and his central theme is about discovering somewhere usually overlooked. The title is 'History, heritage and haute cuisine'.

From there to Summerlee Museum, Coatbridge, it's only a 20-minute drive – 40 minutes with my sense of direction, but this was a place I could not afford to miss. Through a precise guided tour by the museum's Tommy Gallacher, I was given a deep insight into the history and heritage of

Non-fiction

coal mining and steel manufacturing, even stepping deep underground to a reincarnated coal seam . . .

The day was now ended and all that was left for me was to join the happy throng on the M74 and head south. Destination, Biggar – or, at least, a wee village just to the northeast of it called Skirling. There I was rewarded for my day's toil with accommodation in Skirling House, under the caring auspices of Bob and Isobel Hunter. A quick check on the internet only hinted at the attractions of this house, and I would go back like a shot. In fact, both places I stayed, here and in Motherwell, deserve a five-star rating with the Hunters' abode winning by a short head for its informality and excellent service. It was as if you were family who had just popped over to visit, and a Canadian couple and I were given service one would expect from a top-of-the-range city hotel.

The lounge displays a 16th-century ceiling from Florence with 126 carved roses, of which no two are the same. I would still be there if I was to attempt to prove this an idle boast, but a bottle of Greenmantle Ale in front of a roaring fire soon settled me. Okay, the beer comes from the Broughton brewery which is in Peeblesshire and not from Lanarkshire, but who's quibbling? The county boundary is only a quarter of a mile away.

Extract taken from *The Scots Magazine*, November 2012.

Travel

Here's another example, this time from a newspaper travel article. The author, Andrew Cawley, has travelled around the isles of Lewis and Harris and Skye, in the Outer Hebrides of Scotland, in a 1965 Volkswagen campervan, christened Zebedee.

The space restrictions of a small newspaper article create here punchier, more pared down sentences, making the use of clear, concise writing all the more important. The voice used, though, is still chatty and conversational and anecdotes and humour create a sense of the writer's personality. And there is still a wider theme, used to frame the article – appreciating what we have at home, rather than holidaying abroad. The title is 'We fell in love with Zebedee'.

It's about going back to basics. With its four gears, you don't go much faster than 50mph, but when you're meandering your way through magnificent scenery and breathtaking natural beauty, what's the rush? Got-to-be-there-NOW cars will overtake, but hey, let them! And it's guaranteed that when they do overtake, they will always take a long, envious look . . .

This part of the Isle is dominated by the desolate

Non-fiction

expanse of the Black Moor, a vast area of peat bog broken up only by scattered gleaming lochans. The landscape is rugged and weather beaten. Immediately your imagination brings you to wonder what life for islanders was like centuries ago when living was harsh.

The Arnol "Blackhouse" gives a fascinating insight into such traditional times. This perfectly-preserved combined byre, barn and home, with its turf roof and peat-smoke filled walls, gives an evocative glimpse into ancient island life . . .

And this, for me, was what made these islands so special – they are simply so quiet and tranquil. It was easy to relax and forget about all the stress of our modern lives. And there's something just so satisfyingly simple about being able to park up by the beach, cook some food on the BBQ, and sit and watch the sun go down.

When you have the opportunity to experience places like this then for a moment at least nothing else matters.

Extract taken from *The Sunday Post Travel and Homes*, January 13, 2013.

Example of literary travel writing

Despite its differing length and purpose, looking at longer travel literature can be helpful for those who wish to write travel articles. While on a much

Travel

larger scale, these works contain many of the features of a good article: a strong sense of the place and the people and of the writer's personality, evocative description and a wider or over-arching theme which the writer is led into considering by their surroundings and experiences. In an article, however, this theme or idea will not be discussed at length. The focus of the piece, and most of its words, will be on the place visited – which is what readers want to hear about.

Robert Louis Stevenson's *Travels with a Donkey in the Cévennes* is a classic of travel literature. It recounts Stevenson's 12-day, 120-mile hike through the remote, mountainous region of the Cévennes in southern France, aided by his very difficult donkey, Modestine. In this extract, Stevenson has been taught by a local that he needs to use the stick against Modestine, as well as the call 'Proot!', in order to spur her on: a cruelty he is having trouble with. Stevenson's problems with the donkey create some of the wonderful humour which runs through the book.

In this pleasant humour I came down the hill to where Goudet stands in a green end of a valley, with Château

Non-fiction

Beaufort opposite upon a rocky steep, and the stream, as clear as crystal, lying in a deep pool between them. Above and below, you may hear it wimpling over the stones, an amiable stripling of a river, which it seems absurd to call the Loire. On all sides, Goudet is shut in by mountains; rocky footpaths, practicable at best for donkeys, join it to the outer world of France; and the men and women drink and swear, in their green corner, or look up at the snow-clad peaks in winter from the threshold of their homes, in an isolation, you would think, like that of Homer's Cyclops. But it is not so; the postman reaches Goudet with the letter-bag; the aspiring youth of Goudet are within a day's walk of the railway at Le Puy; and here in the inn you may find an engraved portrait of the host's nephew, Régis Senac, 'Professor of Fencing and Champion of the two Americas,' a distinction gained by him, along with the sum of five hundred dollars, at Tammany Hall, New York, on the 10th April 1876.

I hurried over my midday meal, and was early forth again. But, alas, as we climbed the interminable hill upon the other side, 'Proot!' seemed to have lost its virtue. I prooted like a lion, I prooted mellifluously like a sucking-dove; but Modestine would be neither softened nor intimidated. She held doggedly to her pace; nothing but a blow would move her, and that only for a second. I must follow at her heels, incessantly belabouring. A moment's pause in this ignoble toil, and she relapsed into her own private gait. I think I never heard of any one in as mean a situation. I must reach the lake of Bouchet, where I meant to camp, before sundown, and, to have even a hope of this, I must instantly maltreat this uncomplaining animal. The sound of my own blows sickened me. Once, when I looked at her, she had a faint resemblance to a lady of my acquaintance who formerly loaded me with kindness; and this increased my horror of my cruelty.

The full text of this book is available at:
http://www.gutenberg.org/ebooks/535

Travel guides

Writing a travel guide is quite different to writing a travel article. Guides are aimed at tourists or travellers, and their purpose is to provide lots of facts and information about a location or tourist destination.

Many travel guides are published online as travel websites or online guides, rather than in hard copy book format.

There are many different types of travel guides. For example, there are guides that focus on:

Non-fiction

- adventure or activity holidays
- budget holidays
- holidays built around particular interests such as music, art or food.

However, most guide books are meant to be used by the traveller while they are travelling, and contain the following information:

- best time to visit
- history and culture
- maps
- phone numbers, websites, addresses, prices and reviews of hotels and other types of accommodation and places to eat
- entertainment
- places to shop
- key tourist attractions.

It goes without saying that guides have to be written in clear, concise English, and that the facts and figures have to be correct at the time of publication.

Example of a travel guide

Here's an extract from a 'Lonely Planet' travel guide on Venice and the Veneto. The author, Alison Bing, introduces Venice and provides information on arrival and how to get around the city:

ARRIVING IN VENICE

Marco Polo Airport (VCE). Located on the mainland 12km from Venice, east of Mestre. Alilaguna operates ferry service (€13) to Venice from the airport ferry dock (an eight-minute walk from the terminal); expect it to take 45 to 90 minutes to reach most destinations. Water taxis to Venice from airport docks cost €90 to €100. ATVO buses (€5) depart from the airport every 30 minutes from 8am to midnight, and reach Venice's Piazzale Roma within an hour.

Piazzale Roma

This car park is the only point within central Venice accessible by car or bus. *Vaporetto* (water-bus) lines to destinations throughout the city depart from Piazzale Roma docks.

Stazione Santa Lucia

Venice's train station. *Vaporetto* lines depart from Ferrovia (Station) docks.

Stazione Venezia Mestre

Mestre's mainland train station; transfer here to Stazione Santa Lucia.

For much more on **arrival**, see p 250.

GETTING AROUND

Vaporetto

Slow and scenic, the vaporetto is Venice's main public

Non-fiction

transport. Single rides cost €6.50; for frequent use, get a timed pass for unlimited travel within a set period (12/24/36/48/72 hour passes cost €16/18/23/28/33). Tickets, passes and maps are available at dockside Hello-Venezia ticket booths and www.hellovenezia.com.

Extract taken from *Venice and the Veneto (Lonely Planet City Guides)*, by Alison Bing (Lonely Planet Publications, 2012)

Cookery

The shelves of bookshops are full of the latest celebrity cookery books, and they often have websites where you can access their recipes. But you don't have to be a celebrity to write a cookery book or publish your own recipes. Lots of ordinary people love to cook and have tried and tested recipes of their own or special recipes that have been passed down to them that they would like to share.

You might want to produce a collection of your own recipes for a family celebration, or you could collect other people's recipes and publish them for charity, or for a special local event. Whatever the case, you need to think about the following:

Cookery

Theme

Most cookery books are organised around a theme. For example, in many books recipes are organised into starters, main courses, salads and vegetables and desserts. Some books choose a single theme such as fish or seafood dishes, or cooking for a dinner party. Once you have decided what your theme is, the rest will fall into place.

Structure

Recipes usually have a consistent structure, like the following, so the reader knows what to expect:

* title of dish
* how many it serves
* brief description of dish
* ingredients (in order of their appearance in the method)
* method

Here are two different examples:

Two examples of recipe structure

Tomato and Lentil Soup

(serves 4)

This is a hearty and healthy soup, packed full of vitamin C. The lentils give it a satisfying texture. Delicious!

Non-fiction

Ingredients

1 tablespoon of olive oil

1 x medium onion, finely chopped

2 x 400g tins of Italian chopped tomatoes

four cans of water (from empty tins of tomatoes)

one vegetable stock cube

tablespoon of tomato purée

100g of rinsed, no-soak red lentils

Method

- Heat the oil in a medium-sized saucepan.
- Add the onion to the olive oil and fry gently for five minutes, until transparent.
- Now add the two tins of tomatoes, and stir for a further two minutes.
- Add four cans of water (using one of the empty cans of tomatoes).
- Add the stock cube and tomato puree.
- Add the rinsed lentils.
- Bring to the boil, then reduce to a simmer.
- Cook for 20 minutes, then purée and serve.

Sue's Splendid Spaghetti Bolognese

(serves 4)

The title speaks for itself. Cook and enjoy with a glass of Italian red, and feel the sun come out.

Cookery

Ingredients

1 x large onion, finely chopped

1 tbsp of olive oil

2 x cloves garlic, finely chopped

1kg steak mince

2 tsp dried oregano

2 x tins of chopped tomatoes

350ml red wine

beef stock cube

bouquet garni sachet

500g spaghetti (fresh is best)

Method

- Heat the olive oil in a large saucepan.
- Add the onion and garlic and fry gently for five minutes, until transparent.
- Add the mince, and stir until browned.
- Next, add the dried oregano, and stir into the mince.
- Now add the two tins of tomatoes, and stir well.
- Next, add the red wine and the beef stock cube and stir well. Add the bouquet garni sachet.
- Bring the sauce to the boil, then allow to simmer with the lid on for 30 minutes.
- Prepare a large pan of salted water, and cook the spaghetti 5 minutes before the sauce is ready.

Non-fiction

- Serve with green salad, crusty bread and parmesan cheese.

Make sure that you treat measurements consistently – for example, don't mix up imperial and metric measures. And when writing your recipes use either 50 grams or 50g, but not a mixture of both.

Also, a word of warning – ingredients aren't covered by copyright, but the words that are used to describe the method are. So don't plagiarise somebody else's words – use your own.

Photographs

'A picture paints a thousand words.' Successful recipe books all use good photographs to help the reader visualise the finished product, and to make the dish look appetising and appealing. For complicated recipes, involving techniques readers may be unfamiliar with, photographs (or diagrams, if you're of an artistic bent) can also be useful. Step-by-step photos are extremely effective for clarifying and simplifying a technique or entire recipe which would otherwise require a dense, hard-to-follow explanation.

Cookery

Either have a go at taking your own photographs, or ask a professional to take them. Remember that copyright rules also apply to photographs, so don't use somebody else's without getting their permission.

Writing recipes

Writing recipes – especially more complicated or elaborate ones – shares some features in common with technical writing (discussed below). Instructions need to be clear, concise and unambiguous: remember, the reader has to not only understand exactly what you're saying, but also to be able to replicate it themselves. Follow plain English rules.

After writing out a recipe, it helps, rather than just reading it over, to actually go through making the recipe using your instructions, as if making it for the first time. Are any wordings confusing? Are all the techniques involved described as clearly as possible? By doing this, any problems should present themselves more easily. Even better would be to do a trial run of the recipe with a volunteer. Getting someone who hasn't seen the recipe before and who hasn't made the dish before to make it using your recipe is the best test of the

Non-fiction

effectiveness of your writing. Get feedback from them, and adjust accordingly. This is always easier than trying to objectively assess your own words, describing a recipe you are familiar with.

Example of recipe writing

On pages 314–5 there is an example of recipe writing with the use of step-by-step photos, from a book about making macarons, by Jill Colonna.

Macarons, a French delicacy, have a reputation for being complicated to make, and difficult to make well. In writing a recipe book based on the premise that even amateur bakers can make macarons successfully, the author therefore has to be especially skilful in writing her recipes, and careful to follow these rules.

The recipes must be as clear and precise as possible, without being over-complex and putting non-expert readers off. Readers have to be able to thoroughly understand each step in the recipe, while also being confident that they are able to do it.

To avoid the reader feeling overwhelmed with information, Jill breaks down each step into a separate section, along with a photo. This helps not only to make the recipe clearer, but also stops it looking intimidating.

Some tips are presented separately so as not to interrupt the logical sequence of the recipe's steps and to keep directions succinct.

Unfamiliar and foreign terms are used (especially appropriate for a book about a foreign delicacy, assuring readers that they are learning an authentic recipe as well as being interesting), but are translated.

Introductions and other content

You may also wish to include other content besides recipes in your book. Recipe books are not just instructions; they can inspire the reader, give them the thrill of discovering a foreign culture, make them nostalgic or give them a real sense of the life and personality of the author or group who compiled them.

Think about what you are trying to achieve in your recipe book. What tone do you wish to create? While the recipe instructions themselves are succinct and to the point, introductions, to the book and to individual chapters and recipes,

Non-fiction

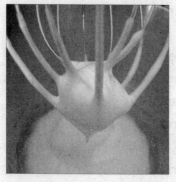

1 Line your three flat baking sheets with perfectly flat greaseproof paper and set aside.

2 Whisk the egg whites (at room temperature) to glossy firm peaks adding the caster sugar gradually. (Tip: ensure the bowl and whisk are perfectly clean. Any trace of fat, yolk or soap will affect the success.)
   If making coloured macarons, then add a dash of colouring (I prefer to use powdered colours or pastes, as less is needed) towards the end of mixing.

EGG TIPS

* To easily separate egg whites from yolks: crack the egg in the middle on the edge of a bowl or another hard surface. With clean hands, over a bowl, gently drop the egg into the palm of one hand, letting the white drip through your fingers into the bowl, leaving the yolk in the palm of your hand.
   No need to waste the yolks: see page 121.

* When making macarons (or meringues) you get the best results from egg whites that have been separated and aged for four to five days in the refrigerator. For 150g of egg white you'll need approximately 5 eggs. Store in a perfectly clean airtight container such as a glass jar.
   Take them out of the fridge 2 hours before use to bring to room temperature.

3 Sift the ground almonds with the icing sugar using a medium sieve. Discard any large, coarse pieces of ground almonds.
   (Tip: if there are a lot of large pieces to discard, weigh them and replace them in the mixture with more ground almonds to make sure you still have the 180g specified.)

   For chocolate macarons (as I am making here) also sift in the 10g of cocoa at this point.

25

Extract from *Mad About Macarons* by Jill Colonna (Waverley Books, 2010).

4   Mix well to incorporate icing sugar and almonds (and cocoa powder if you are using it).

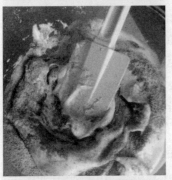

5   Incorporate the beaten egg whites into the dry ingredients using a large spatula. Mix well.

(Note that there is no need to "fold" the mixture.)

6   Then work on the mixture (*macaronnage*) using a plastic scraper (*corne en plastique*). Press down well with the scraper, going back and forward, to press out the oxygen from the whites. Do this for no more than 5 minutes until you have a smooth mixture.

(It helps if your bowl is flat in the middle.)

26

commentaries and fact boxes can all be used to create a sense of personality and individuality, as well as to provide information. On the next page is an extract from the introduction to *Mad About Macarons* by Jill Colonna (Waverley Books, 2010).

The author talks about her own background and first encounter with macarons. By telling us about her history she gives us a sense of why she is qualified to write a book about macarons.

We learn that she has lived in France for twenty years, that she has long been passionate about French baking and that the macaron, for her, was an immediate love affair.

This also individualises the book: we get a real sense of the author's own voice, and who she is. On top of this, her story of her first discovery of French pâtisseries really sets the scene for the book.

We are given an insight into the culture surrounding macarons, and into French culture in general, and a sense of atmosphere is created. This gets the reader into the right frame of mind, leaving them enthused and eager to get started on the recipes!

Cookery

Discovering the Macaron
AND DISCOVERING I COULD MAKE MY OWN

When I came to live in France nearly 20 years ago I didn't have a sweet tooth. Dessert was just an apple and some cheese. But the beckoning Parisian pâtisseries had me quickly lured in by their sophisticated window displays and I was converted. How can you resist a perfectly presented delicacy called *un mille feuille* (a thousand leaves), crammed with fragrant vanilla custard cream between flaky, toasted layers of pastry under an artistic icing?

Suddenly I felt so far away from our local baker in Edinburgh who produced something similar, but called it a *mayo fayo* with a posh accent. I wanted to practise this new mouthful, repeating "un mille feuille, s'il vous plaît" in so many pâtisseries until I discovered the best cakes in our Parisian *arrondissement* and until I was no longer snootily corrected for my atrocious French accent. There was so much to learn.

After tasting my way through the pâtisserie classics using my student lunch money, it was finally a relief to be a working girl, working in Paris, in a château, in a chic part of town.

Occasionally I could indulge in the opulence of a *salon de thé* (tea salon), drinking tea from a porcelain cup. It was fascinating: like having afternoon tea in a grand hotel's palm court but without the piano or the sandwiches. The women were so stylish and slim! French women don't eat between meals. They are so strict at sticking to mealtimes. I had a friend who if she missed lunch was so disciplined that she would not eat until her tea and gâteau at 4 o'clock. They eat well and they stay slim.

Ten years ago, macarons were not in most pâtisseries as they are now in Paris. It was in Paris that I discovered the macaron. It was during a lunch break with the girls at the salon de thé on the top floor of a seriously classy ladies' department store in the 16th arrondissement. The macaron was on all the elegant ladies' plates like a fashion accessory.

It was love at first sight: they were perfection on a porcelain plate, so airy and delicate that you didn't feel like you'd have to play at dress sizes if you became hooked, yet they were just big enough to savour and appreciate their sweet voluptuous perfumed centre with a refreshing cuppa.

They looked so perfect and dainty and certainly not something you could obviously make at home. That was for the professionals, I thought.

317

Non-fiction

Technical writing

Technical writers communicate technical, scientific, legal, mechanical or business information to other people who might or might not be familiar with these fields. If you have ever successfully assembled a piece of furniture, or installed a DVD player, then you will have read and (hopefully!) understood technical writing. Technical writers are currently in high demand to explain, review and promote the new technological products that are constantly being developed and produced. There are three main types of technical writing:

- **end-user documents** – where the writer explains technical information to non-technical people in a way that is easy to understand and follow
- **traditional technical writing** – for example, in engineering and science, written specifically for an audience that is already familiar with the field
- **technological marketing material** – as in fliers and promotional leaflets that persuade people to buy a technological product or service.

First, we will explore the main characteristics of all of these types of technical writing. We will then look in more detail at what each of these types of writing involves by giving examples.

Successful technical writing – no matter what the subject – has the following characteristics:

- it is clear, concise and unambiguous – a lot of technical writing is for non-technical people, and they have to be able to understand it
- it doesn't include too much technical language – unless this is appropriate for the intended audience, who already know and understand this
- it is objective
- it clearly refers to contributions already made by others in the field – this is more the case in the traditional technical writing field
- it is accurate and complete – getting it wrong or missing something out could at best be annoying but at worst be dangerous – especially if it's a safety or instruction manual.

In the pages that follow are examples of the three different types of technical writing mentioned opposite.

Get Started! The Beginner's Guide to Computers

A peripheral allows you to communicate with your computer. There are two types: those which provide **input** and enable you to tell the computer what you want it to do (such as the keyboard and mouse) and those which display **output** such as the monitor or printer.

Input

The keyboard

The keyboard is one of the main ways in which you will send instructions and data to your computer. It has several types of key. There are letter, number and punctuation keys which are similar to those of a typewriter – holding down **Shift** while keying a letter gives you a capital, while pressing **Enter** (Return) starts a new paragraph.

Along the top of the keyboard are **function keys** (F1-F12) which do different things in different programs but F1 is usually a link to the Help facility.

There are also **navigational** or **arrow keys** to help you move around the screen, a **numeric keypad** to make it easier when you are keying in figures, and various special keys such as Control, Alt and the Windows keys.

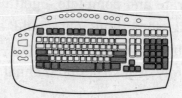

Fig. 1.2 A standard keyboard with main key types highlighted

From *The Beginner's Guide to Computers* by David McCormick (Geddes & Grosset, 2010).

Technical writing

End-user documents

Examples of end-user documents range from a computer manual to an instruction leaflet to help you assemble a piece of furniture.

Examples of end-user documents

The example on page 320 is taken from *The Beginner's Guide to Computers* by David McCormick (Geddes & Grosset, 2010). The guide starts with the most basic information and builds to more advanced information, ensuring that the user feels confident with every new section. Subsections are short, with each separate topic being given a new subheading, and the wider sections are clearly defined and move logically. Figures are used, as well as screenshots of programs, and major terms are put in bold on their first use to effectively signpost information.

The second example on page 322 is taken from a software instruction manual. Software manuals need to explain things simply and in an accessible way. They need to cover all eventualities to accomodate users who may know nothing, but also have an index or contents page that enables a more experienced user to quickly reach the information they need.

Sample Model: Party

This activity gets you thinking about computer modeling and how you can use it. It also gives you insight into NetLogo itself. We encourage beginning users to start here.

At a Party

Have you ever been at a party and noticed how people cluster in groups? You may have also noticed that people don't just stay in a group. As they circulate, the groups change. If you watched these changes over time, you might notice patterns.

For example, in social settings, people may exhibit different behavior than at work or home. Individuals who are confident within their work environment may become shy and timid at a social gathering. And others who are reserved at work may be the "party starter" with friends.

These patterns can depend on the type of gathering. In some settings, people are trained to organize themselves into mixed groups; for example, party games or school-like activities. But in a non-structured atmosphere, people tend to group in a more random manner.

Is there any type of pattern to this kind of grouping?

Let's take a closer look at this question by using the computer to model human behavior at a party. NetLogo's "Party" model looks specifically at the question of grouping by gender at parties: why do groups tend to form that are mostly men, or mostly women?

Let's use NetLogo to explore this question.

What to do:

1. Start NetLogo.
2. Choose "Models Library" from the File menu.

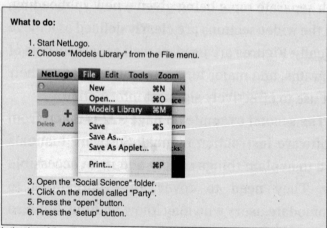

3. Open the "Social Science" folder.
4. Click on the model called "Party".
5. Press the "open" button.
6. Press the "setup" button.

In the view of the model, you will see pink and blue groups with numbers:

Sample Model: Party

Extract from the *NetLogo* manual by U Wilensky (Northwestern University, Evanston, IL.)

Technical writing

Software manuals – and instruction manuals in general – are therefore a difficult thing to produce. When it is done correctly we readers will not even notice. However, when you encounter a bad instruction manual you know it. Your frustration levels are a big clue!

The sample we've included is from a manual for a piece of software called NetLogo. (Wilensky, U [1999]. http://ccl.northwestern.edu/netlogo/. Center for Connected Learning and Computer-Based Modeling, Northwestern University, Evanston, IL.)

The end user is given an introductory overview and examples to try to help explain in simple terms what the software does and why it does it that way.

Traditional technical writing

Examples of traditional technical writing are also wide ranging. For example, they could include an article that has been written and published in a medical journal such as *The Lancet* or a paper published in an engineering journal about an innovative system or piece of product design.

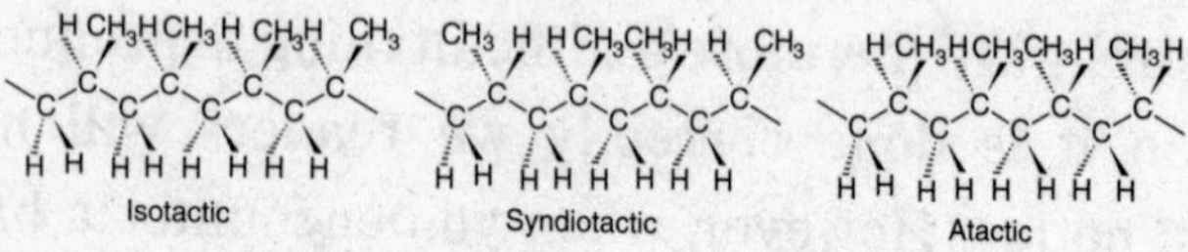

Figure 2.3 *Three tactic forms of polypropylene.*

radical initiated polymerisation this is difficult. However in the 1950s Zeigler and Natta discovered that it was possible to initiate the polymerisation of propylene using solid state catalysts. The catalysts created using aluminium trialkyl and titanium tetrachloride produced a polymer in which chiral control had been achieved at the reaction centre. So we now refer to the stereochemistry of the resulting polymer as its *tacticity*. If all the groups adding to the active centre give the same chirality, the polymer is termed *isotactic*. As an example we can consider polypropylene (Figure 2.3).

If the monomers add in an alternating manner, the polymer is termed *syndio-tactic*. Polymers without any control of the chiral addition, which is the case for normal free radical polymerisation, are termed *atactic*. The physical properties of polymers prepared with and without stereochemical control can be very different. For example, isotactic polypropylene is a hard crystalline material and can be used to make pipes used in domestic hot water systems, whereas the syndiotactic and atactic polymers are soft tacky materials, which are used as thickening agents for lubricating oils and as components in adhesives.

2.5 Geometric isomerism

In the case of important elastomers formed by polymerisation of conjugated dienes, addition across one double bond can, by electron migration, cause movement of the second double bond. This results in either 1,2 or 1,4 addition across the four-carbon monomer (Figure 2.4).

So polybutadiene can be obtained with different physical characteristics, depending on the conditions used in its synthesis. Simple addition to the first vinyl bond leads to the 1,2 addition product. This polymer is rigid at room temperature compared with the 1,4 addition product, which is rubbery. Furthermore 1,4 addition can create either *trans* or *cis* configurations, and these can have different degrees of local order.

Extract from *Introduction to Molecular Motion in Polymers* by Richard A Pethrick, Taweechai Amornsakchai and Alistair M North [Whittles Publishing, 2011].

Example of traditional technical writing

The example on page 324 is from the book *Introduction to Molecular Motion in Polymers*. It is written specifically for an audience that understands this scientific field and its language, so if you don't understand it all, that's not surprising. It also clearly cites other people's contributions.

The extract is taken from *Introduction to Molecular Motion in Polymers* (Richard A Pethrick, Taweechai Amornsakchai and Alistair M North [Whittles Publishing, 2011]).

Technological marketing material

You can't escape examples of technological marketing materials. They are everywhere, from TV and radio adverts to billboard posters to websites and blogs.

We are constantly bombarded with materials that are trying to persuade us to buy a certain type of computer, tablet or phone, because it has technological features that make it much better than the previous model.

Copywriters for technological marketing materials will in general try to:

Non-fiction

- Speak directly to a target audience they (or the company) have in mind. They will keep this person in mind as they write.

- Focus on what's in it for the reader/listener/ viewer – why they should want to buy the product. It doesn't matter how great or sophisticated or clever the product is if it doesn't offer something for them: solve a problem they face, or improve their life in some way.

- Be careful to talk on the right level for the person they're speaking to in their marketing copy. Technological details given have to be comprehensible for them and to be relevant to them and what they would seek in a product. Going into dense, over-complicated explanations of the technology involved wouldn't convince a reader of how clever a product is; it would just make them stop reading.

'How to' writing

'How to' writing is slightly different to technical writing. It assumes that readers are non-experts, and it tells or instructs them how to accomplish a specific task or change certain behaviours or attitudes.

There are lots of 'how to' publications or textbooks in the business, 'self-help' and hobbies sections of bookshops, libraries and websites.

'How to' writing tends to have the following characteristics. It:

- has an informal and conversational style and tone – 'you' and 'we' rather than 'he', 'she' and 'it'
- contains hints, tips and anecdotes
- is clear, concise and accessible
- is easy to understand
- assumes no prior knowledge of the topic.

Examples of 'how to' writing

The 'For Dummies' series is a very well-known collection of 'how to' books on just about every topic you could think of – from *Cricket for Dummies* to *Statistics for Dummies* to *Baby and Toddler Sleep Solutions for Dummies*.

Non-fiction

The books consistently stick to the same format. They have a very clear table of contents, so the reader knows immediately what the book is about. They also have frequent headings to signpost information and are written concisely in plain English. They usually assume no prior knowledge of the subject, and they have an informal style.

On the following pages is an example of 'how to' writing from the book *Yoga and Meditation*, by Katherine Wright, published by Geddes & Grosset, 2007. It's an introductory text with step-by-step instructions and clear and simple illustrations.

This is a piece of writing geared towards people who are not experts in yoga or meditation. It isn't explaining any particularly complicated concepts, but it is clearly and concisely explaining to readers how to carry out the yoga moves and meditation techniques.

Examples, diagrams and figures are used in order to give readers a better understanding of processes that might be unfamiliar. Diagrams are used to illuminate the textual description. The figures are simple enough to be intelligible to non-experts.

Paragraphs are quite short, and there are lots

Yoga and Meditation

Easy posture

Easy posture

Basically, this involves sitting cross-legged with both feet on the floor. The back should be straight but not tense and the stomach muscles relaxed. With the muscles of the lower back bearing the weight of the body and with the head, neck and trunk in line, the centre of gravity passes from the base of the spine right through the top of the head. The hands can either be resting lightly on the knees or held in the lap, either one on top of the other or clasped lightly.

Siddhasana

Sitting on the floor with the back straight, stretch the legs out in front of you. Bend the left knee and, grasping the left foot with both hands, draw it towards the body until the heel is resting against the part of the lower body that lies between

54

Chapter 4 – How to Begin

Siddhasana

the anus and genitalia. Now draw the right foot towards the body until the heel is on the pubic bone. Tuck the toes of the right foot between the calf and the thigh of the left leg. Rest the hands, palms upwards on the knees. Siddhasana is sometimes called the perfect posture.

Seven-point posture

1   If possible, try to sit with the legs crossed in the lotus position, or varja, with each foot placed sole upwards on the thigh of the opposite leg. To get into the lotus position loosen up with the exercises on pages 63–70 and then sit on the floor, legs stretched out in front of you. Now bend the right knee and, grasping the right foot with both hands, place it on top of the left thigh, heel pressing into the abdomen. Repeat the process with the left foot.

55

'How to' writing

of headings and sub-headings, splitting the text into manageable sections.

Other 'how to' books show many of the same techniques. Here's an example from a book on raising teenagers called *Surviving Teenagers* by Dr David Fong (Geddes & Grosset, 2007).

Stuck record technique

A technique that many parents find helpful when discussing things with their children is the 'stuck record' technique. It can often be the case in conflicts, that the actual point of the discussion gets lost in the heated argument. The stuck record technique is really a way of keeping 'on-message' and avoiding the debate getting too emotionally charged.

For example:

Daughter: Dad, can I borrow the car tonight to go and see Paul?

Dad: Sorry, hon, you know I need it tonight.

Daughter: But it's really, really important that I use the car!

Dad: I'm sorry, but you know I need the car every Tuesday night.

Daughter: Couldn't you just let me have it this once? It's really important!

Non-fiction

Dad: Sorry, it's Tuesday and I need it.

Daughter: That's just typical! You just won't see how important this is for me, will you? You're so selfish!

Dad: Yep, I am selfish, it is still Tuesday and I need the car.

Now Dad has to use this technique with care – if he knows for example, that he doesn't really need the car and he's just being mean then this technique has been misused. If, on the other hand, he has made it perfectly clear that on Tuesdays the car is off limits then this technique can be helpful. It avoids the discussion of whether Dad is selfish or not, what is typical or not and it keeps to the point about who is using the car.

Extract taken from *Surviving Teenagers* by Dr David Fong, (Geddes & Grosset, 2007)

The heading at the beginning of this extract signposts the example so it can easily be referred back to later. Language is clear, concise and informal. (Imagine the change in tone if 'Dad' was replaced with 'The father', or if the example conversation was replaced with a more prescriptive paragraph of instruction ['the father must now', 'the father must not'].) The example conversation also gets the author's point across much more clearly and economically than a lengthy description of the technique would have.

On the two following pages is another example of an accessible 'how to' book. In the book *Quit Smoking* by Dr David Fong (Geddes & Grosset, 2007), the author adopts a conversational tone that is informal and easy to read and understand. He also uses anecdotes from life to illustrate his points. The book is split into distinct sections, each dealing with a single topic, which is summarised in the section title. Look at the detailed table of contents on the next few pages.

In *Quit Smoking*, signposting is key to the organisation of the book. Chapters are numbered, but are also titled with a key sentence relating to that chapter's content. This is followed by a subtitle which summarises the chapter. Subsections are also clearly titled with their subject and move in a logical progression.

There are diagrams and drawings in this book, adding to the information given by the text and also providing humour. A little humour is what's needed for such a task as quitting smoking!

Contents

5

Pages 334–7, contents pages from Quit Smoking by Dr David Fong (Geddes & Grosset, 2007)

6

Contents

7

Contents

9

Non-fiction

The next two pages show an example of an entirely different type of 'how to' writing. This is taken from a book called *It's Not Rocket Science: Learn to Swim* (Waverley Books, 2012).

This combines many of the aspects of technical writing with those of 'how to' writing. Swimming, as a complex set of physical movements, is a hard thing to explain clearly and logically in writing, in a way that can be not only understood but replicated by readers.

Descriptions need to be broken down as much as possible into individual steps. Language needs to be clear, concise and, crucially, unambiguous. Steps need to be listed in a logical progression. This description is aided by the use of figures (as with technical writing), as well as by the structure of the sections.

Each section deals with a separate part of the swimming stroke being described, is clearly labelled, and has relevant names for phases and movements involved in the stroke in bold.

Finally, this book – *Better English Writing* – is an example of a 'how to' text. Hopefully it will help you to understand how to write better English in all aspects of your life and work!

b) During **the pull** you should try to keep your hand fairly close to the body whether you are on your front or your back (figure 12). Your elbow will be bent and you will feel, just like climbing a rope, that you are pulling your body over the top of your hand.

Figure 12: The pull used for the crawl

c) Recovery action is the last phase of the crawl stroke. Here your elbow should be bent and your arm recovered quickly towards your front ready for re-entry. But it should be done in such a way that your recovery arm does not interfere with your other arm, which is pulling (figure 13). These principles apply on your front and on your back.

Pages 339 and 340 from *It's Not Rocket Science: Learn to Swim* (Waverley Books, 2012)

Figure 13: Recovery in the crawl

Breaststroke arm action

The breaststroke action begins in the stretch starting position with both your hands together and your arms straight. From there your hands pull backwards in a circling movement (see figure 14 on page 34). Try not to pull beyond the line of your shoulders as this will cause your head and the top part of your body to submerge. Just pull to the line of the shoulders, then your elbows bend coming in under your chest, and your arms stretch forward in recovery.

Reference works

You consult general reference materials for specific information – you don't need to read them all the way through like you would a novel.

Examples of general reference books or materials include the following:

- dictionary
- thesaurus
- encyclopedia
- atlas
- directory

All of the above help you to find or research specific information, or point you to somewhere else that you can find it.

You probably won't have to write anything for a reference book, because a lot of this type of writing is very specialised. For example, lexicography is the art of compiling, writing and editing dictionaries, and is usually undertaken by experts trained in the field. The actual writing and editing of dictionaries is called practical lexicography. The analysis or description of the vocabulary and how words link to others is known as theoretical lexicography.

Non-fiction

However, you will probably have to use some or all of these reference materials if you are researching or writing material of your own. Search engines, such as Google, have their place but they won't always direct you to the specific information or answers you need. It's therefore useful to know what these reference materials are, how they can help you and how you can get the most out of them.

Dictionary

A dictionary is an essential tool for anybody who is writing anything. A dictionary provides definitions of words in alphabetical order. Sometimes they provide information about the pronunciation and the etymology (or origin – for example, Latin or Greek) of the word. Dictionaries come in different formats, including books, electronic devices, websites and word processing tools.

Here are six well-known dictionaries:

- *The Oxford English Dictionary*
- *The Cambridge Business English Dictionary*
- *The Chambers Dictionary*
- *Collins English Dictionary*
- *Macmillan Dictionary*
- *Merriam-Webster Dictionary*

Reference works

There are also lots of online dictionaries available.

Example of how to use a dictionary

On page 344 there is an example of how you would use a dictionary and on page 345 an extract from a dictionary.

Say that you want to know what the definition of 'psychology' is. You're also not completely sure how to spell it. How do you find it?

You know it begins with 'p', so you turn first to that section of the alphabet in the dictionary.

You think it's followed by a 'y', but you quickly realise after searching for words under 'py' that this is wrong.

You know that there's an 's' in it somewhere, so you search next under 'psy', and you quickly find a number of similar-sounding words such as 'psychiatry' and 'psycho'.

You read down the list of words and bingo! you arrive at 'psychology'.

There are two definitions listed for this word:
1. the study of the human mind.
2. the mental processes of a person.

provocative /pru-**voc**-a-tiv/ adj intended to anger or annoy, arousing the emotions or passions.

provoke /pru-**voke**/ vb 1 to make angry. 2 to give rise to.

prow /prow/ n the front part of a ship or boat.

prowess /prow-ess/ n skill or ability.

prowl /prowl/ vb to keep moving about as if searching for something, to move quietly about looking for the chance to do mischief.

prowler /prow-ler/ n someone who moves stealthily, especially a thief.

proximate /prok-si-mit/ adj (fml) nearest.

proximity /prok-**si**-mi-tee/ n nearness, neighbourhood.

proxy /prok-see/ n 1 the right to act or vote for another. 2 someone with the right to act or vote for another.

prude /prood/ n a person who makes a show of being very modest and correct in behaviour. • n **prudery.**

prudence /proo-dense/ n foresight, caution.

prudent /proo-dent/ adj thinking carefully before acting, wise, cautious.

prudery see **prude.**

prudish /proo-dish/ adj over-correct in behaviour.

prune[1] /proon/ n a dried plum.

prune[2] /proon/ vb 1 to cut off the dead or overgrown parts of a plant. 2 to shorten by cutting out what is unnecessary.

pry /prie/ vb to inquire closely, especially into the secrets of others; to examine closely.

psalm /sahm/ n a sacred song or hymn.

psalmist /sahm-ist/ n a writer of sacred songs.

pseudo /soo-doe/ adj false, not real.

pseudonym /soo-du-nim/ n a name used instead of one's real name (e.g. a pen-name).

psychiatry /sie-kie-u-tree/ n the treatment of diseases of the mind. • n **psychiatrist.**

psychic /sie-kik/, **psychical** /sie-ki-kal/ adj 1 having to do with the mind. 2 (of influences and forces) that act on the mind and senses but have no physical cause. 3 (of a person) sensitive to these influences. 4 able to communicate with spirits. • n someone who claims to be psychic, a clairvoyant.

psychoanalysis /sie-ko-a-**na**-li-sis/ n treatment of mental disease by questioning problems, fears, etc, that exist in the patient's mind without his or her being aware of them. • n **psychoanalyst.** • vb **psychoanalyse.**

psychology /sie-kol-u-jee/ n 1 the study of the human mind. 2 the mental processes of a person. • adj **psychological.** • n **psychologist.**

psychopath /sie-ko-path/ n someone with a personality disorder which can lead him or her to commit often violent acts without guilt.

pterodactyl /ter-u-**dac**-tul/ n a prehistoric winged reptile known of from fossils.

pub /pub/ n a building in which alcoholic drinks, and sometimes food, are served; a public house.

puberty /pyoo-bur-tee/ n the age by which a young person has fully developed all the characteristics of his or her sex.

public /pu-blic/ adj 1 open to all. 2 having to do with people in general. 3 well-known. • n the people in general.

publication /pu-bli-**cay**-shun/ n 1 the act of publishing. 2 a published book, magazine or paper.

public house /pub-lick howss/ see **pub.**

public school /pub-lick skool/ n 1 in England, a fee-paying private school for senior pupils who often live at the school. 2 in US and Scotland, a free government-run school.

publicity /pu-**bli**-si-tee/ n 1 making something widely known, advertising. 2 the state of being well-known. • vb **publicize,** also **publicise.**

publish /pu-blish/ vb 1 (fml) to make widely known. 2 to print for selling to the public.

publisher /pu-bli-sher/ n someone who publishes books, etc.

puck /puck/ n a small hard rubber disc used instead of a ball in ice hockey.

pucker /pu-ker/ vb to gather into small folds or wrinkles. • n a fold or wrinkle.

pudding /poo-ding/ n a sweet soft dessert served at the end of a meal.

puddle /pu-dul/ n a small pool of dirty water. • vb to make watertight with clay.

pudgy /pu-jee/ adj (inf) short and fat.

puff /puff/ n 1 a short sharp breath or gust of wind. 2 a small cloud of smoke, steam, etc, blown by a puff. 3 a soft pad for powdering the skin. 4 a kind of light pastry. • vb 1 to breathe quickly or heavily, as when short of breath. 2 to blow in small blasts. 3 to blow up, to swell. 4 to praise too highly.

puffin /pu-fin/ n a diving bird with a brightly coloured beak.

puffy /pu-fee/ adj blown out, swollen.

pug, pug dog /pug dawg/ n a type of small dog with an upturned nose.

pugnacious /pug-**nay**-shus/ adj quarrelsome, fond of fighting. • n **pugnacity.**

pug nose /pug noze/ n a short upturned nose. • adj **pug-nosed.**

puke /pyook/ vb (inf) to bring up the contents of the stomach, to vomit.

pule /pyool/ vb (fml) to whine, to cry peevishly.

Here is one example of how a dictionary page is put together:

Elements in the Dictionary

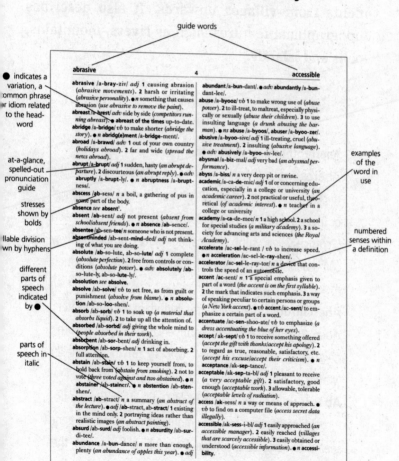

guide words

● indicates a variation, a common phrase or idiom related to the head-word

at-a-glance, spelled-out pronunciation guide

stresses shown by bolds

syllable division shown by hyphens

different parts of speech indicated by ●

parts of speech in italic

examples of the word in use

numbered senses within a definition

abrasive /a-bray-ziv/ *adj* **1** causing abrasion (*abrasive movements*). **2** harsh or irritating (*abrasive personality*). ● *n* something that causes abrasion (*use abrasive to remove the paint*).

abreast /a-brest/ *adv* side by side (*competitors running abreast*). ● **abreast of the times** up-to-date.

abridge /a-bridge/ *vb* to make shorter (*abridge the story*). ● *n* **abridg(e)ment** /a-bridge-ment/.

abroad /a-brawd/ *adv* **1** out of your own country (*holidays abroad*). **2** far and wide (*spread the news abroad*).

abrupt /a-brupt/ *adj* **1** sudden, hasty (*an abrupt departure*). **2** discourteous (*an abrupt reply*). ● *adv* **abruptly** /a-brupt-ly/. ● *n* **abruptness** /a-bruptness/.

abscess /ab-sess/ *n* a boil, a gathering of pus in some part of the body.

absence *see* **absent**[1].

absent /ab-sent/ *adj* not present (*absent from school/absent friends*). ● *n* **absence** /ab-sence/.

absentee /ab-sen-tee/ *n* someone who is not present.

absentminded /ab-sent-mind-ded/ *adj* not thinking of what you are doing.

absolute /ab-so-lute, ab-so-lute/ *adj* **1** complete (*absolute perfection*). **2** free from controls or conditions (*absolute power*). ● *adv* **absolutely** /ab-so-lute-ly, ab-so-lute-ly/.

absolution *see* **absolve**.

absolve /ab-solve/ *vb* to set free, as from guilt or punishment (*absolve from blame*). ● *n* **absolution** /ab-so-loo-shen/.

absorb /ab-sorb/ *vb* **1** to soak up (*a material that absorbs liquid*). **2** to take up all the attention of.

absorbed /ab-sorbd/ *adj* giving the whole mind to (*people absorbed in their work*).

absorbent /ab-sor-bent/ *adj* drinking in.

absorption /ab-sorp-shen/ *n* **1** act of absorbing. **2** full attention.

abstain /ab-stain/ *vb* **1** to keep yourself from, to hold back from (*abstain from smoking*). **2** not to vote (*three voted against and two abstained*). ● *n* **abstainer** /ab-stainer/. ● *n* **abstention** /ab-stenshen/.

abstract /ab-stract/ *n* a summary (*an abstract of the lecture*). ● *adj* /ab-stract, ab-stract/ **1** existing in the mind only. **2** portraying ideas rather than realistic images (*an abstract painting*).

absurd /ab-surd/ *adj* foolish. ● *n* **absurdity** /ab-sur-di-tee/.

abundance /a-bun-dance/ *n* more than enough, plenty (*an abundance of apples this year*). ● *adj*

abundant /a-bun-dant/. ● *adv* **abundantly** /a-bun-dant-lee/.

abuse /a-byooz/ *vb* **1** to make wrong use of (*abuse power*). **2** to ill-treat, to maltreat, especially physically or sexually (*abuse their children*). **3** to use insulting language (*a drunk abusing the barman*). ● *ns* **abuse** /a-byoos/, **abuser** /a-byoo-zer/.

abusive /a-byoo-sive/ *adj* **1** ill-treating, cruel (*abusive treatment*). **2** insulting (*abusive language*). ● *adv* **abusively** /a-byoo-siv-lee/.

abysmal /a-biz-mal/ *adj* very bad (*an abysmal performance*).

abyss /a-biss/ *n* a very deep pit or ravine.

academic /a-ca-de-mic/ *adj* **1** of or concerning education, especially in a college or university (*an academic career*). **2** not practical or useful, theoretical (*of academic interest*). ● *n* teacher in a college or university

academy /a-ca-de-mee/ *n* **1** a high school. **2** a school for special studies (*a military academy*). **3** a society for advancing arts and sciences (*the Royal Academy*).

accelerate /ac-sel-le-rant/ *vb* to increase speed. ● *n* **acceleration** /ac-sel-le-ray-shen/.

accelerator /ac-sel-le-ray-tor/ *n* a device that controls the speed of an automobile.

accent /ac-sent/ *n* **1** special emphasis given to part of a word (*the accent is on the first syllable*). **2** the mark that indicates such emphasis. **3** a way of speaking peculiar to certain persons or groups (*a New York accent*). ● *vb* **accent** /ac-sent/ to emphasize a certain part of a word.

accentuate /ac-sen-shoo-ate/ *vb* to emphasize (*a dress accentuating the blue of her eyes*).

accept /ak-sept/ *vb* **1** to receive something offered (*accept the gift with thanks/accept his apology*). **2** to regard as true, reasonable, satisfactory, etc. (*accept his excuse/accept their criticism*). ● *n* **acceptance** /ak-sep-tance/.

acceptable /ak-sep-ta-bl/ *adj* **1** pleasant to receive (*a very acceptable gift*). **2** satisfactory, good enough (*acceptable work*). **3** allowable, tolerable (*acceptable levels of radiation*).

access /ak-sess/ *n* a way or means of approach. ● *vb* to find on a computer file (*access secret data illegally*).

accessible /ak-sess-i-bl/ *adj* **1** easily approached (*an accessible manager*). **2** easily reached (*villages that are scarcely accessible*). **3** easily obtained or understood (*accessible information*). ● *n* **accessibility**.

abrasive   4   **accessible**

Non-fiction

Other types of dictionaries

There are also other types of dictionaries. Here are two extracts taken from a dictionary of names that includes virtually all of Scotland's settlements from villages upwards. It also describes topographical features such as rivers, mountains, lochs and islands:

A

Aberbrothock *see* **Arbroath**.

Abercairney (Perth & Kinross) 'Confluence by the thicket' or 'cairns'. *Aber* (Brythonic-Pictish) 'confluence' or 'river mouth'; *cardden* (Brythonic) 'thicket'; with *-ach* (Scottish Gaelic suffix) indicating 'place'; or alternatively *càirneach* (Scottish Gaelic) 'place of cairns or rough rocks'.

Aberchirder (Aberdeenshire) 'Mouth of the dark water'. *Aber* (Brythonic-Pictish) 'confluence' or 'river mouth'; *chiar* (Scottish Gaelic) 'dark'; *dobhar* (Brythonic-Gaelic) 'waters'.

Aberdeen 'Mouth of the River Don'. *Aber* (Brythonic-Pictish) 'confluence' or 'river mouth'; the second element seems to suggest the River Dee, which flows into the North Sea at the centre of modern Aberdeen, but the name was recorded as Aberdon in the early 12th century and at that time referred to the original settlement now known as Old Aberdeen, situated immediately to the north at the mouth of the River Don, close to the Cathedral of St Machar. By the 13th century, the current name form, probably a conflation of the two, was emerging as Aberdoen in 1178 and Aberden in 1214. *See also* **Rivers Dee** and **Don**.

Aberdour (Fife) 'Mouth of the River Dour'. *Aber* (Brythonic-Pictish) 'confluence' or 'river mouth'; . . .

T

Tain (Highland) 'Water'. This old royal burgh, once a pilgrimage place to St Duthac's shrine, stands at the mouth of a small river, the Tain Water. Once thought to be Norse, the name is now ascribed to a Pre-Celtic root-form indicating 'river' or 'water'. It is recorded as: Tene in 1227, Tayne in 1375 and Thane in 1483.

Taing This very common name along the Orkney and Shetland coasts is from the Old Norse *thang,* indicating 'a low headland'.

Talisker (Highland) 'Sloping Rock'. *T-hallr* (Old Norse) 'sloping'; *skjaer* (Old Norse) 'rock'.

Non-fiction

Talla (Borders) 'The brow'. *Talg* (Brythonic) 'front' or 'brow'.

Tanera (Highland) 'Harbour isle'. *T-h-fnar* (Old Norse) 'harbour'; *ey* (Old Norse) 'isle'. There are two Taneras in the Summer Isles, differentiated in Gaelic as *Mór*, 'big' and *Beag*, 'small'.

Tankerness (Orkney) 'Tancred's cape'. *Tancred* (Old Norse and Norman personal name); *nes* (Old Norse) 'headland' or 'cape'.

Tantallon (East Lothian) 'High-fronted fort'. *Din* (Brythonic) 'fort'; *talgan* (Brythonic) 'of the high front' or 'of the high brow'.

Taransay (Western Isles) 'Isle of (St) Taran'. *Taran* (Pictish personal name); *ey* (Old Norse) 'island'.

Tarbat Ness (Highland) 'Cape of the isthmus'. *Tairbeart* (Scottish Gaelic) 'isthmus' or 'portage point'; *nes* (Old Norse) 'cape' or 'headland'.

Extracts taken from *Scottish Place Names* by George Mackay (Geddes & Grosset, 2003).

Thesaurus

A thesaurus is another useful tool. You use it to search for words that are similar to (synonyms) or the opposite of (antonyms) other words. It can help you to look for words or phrases that are similar to or mean the exact opposite of the one you have thought of so that you can choose the word or phrase that is best for your purpose.

Example of a thesaurus

Below is an extract from of a thesaurus. You want to describe somebody as a nice, pleasant person, but 'nice' is a very overused word and you are looking for something a bit more interesting. If you look up 'nice' this is the kind of thing you will get:

---

nibble *vb* (*mice nibbling on a piece of cheese*) bite, gnaw, munch.

nice *adj* **1** (*His father is a nice person*) pleasant, friendly, kind, agreeable, charming. **2** (*We had a nice time at the theatre*) pleasant, enjoyable, delightful. **3** (*It was a nice day for the wedding*) fine, sunny, dry. **4** (*There is a nice distinction in meaning between the two words*) fine, subtle, minute, precise.

night *n* (*when night fell*) night-time, darkness, dark. ▼

---

a night owl someone who is in the habit of staying up very late at night (*She is a real night owl. She rarely goes to bed before 2 a.m.*).

Word Power English Thesaurus by Betty Kirkpatrick (Geddes & Grosset, 2013)

Non-fiction

Encyclopedia

An encyclopedia is a book, or series of books, that covers a wide range of topics and subjects. You can access encyclopedias in libraries or in some cases in digital format online.

An encyclopedia is a starting point for facts about a topic, and often includes illustrations, maps and photographs. Most are organised alphabetically, some by category and sometimes entries are cross-referenced. There are some examples of encyclopedic entries on pages 351 and 352.

In very complex volumes there may also be an index. So, for example, if you wanted to know about the pyramids and the gods and goddesses of ancient Egypt, you would search in the index under 'Egypt', and then look for the category of 'Ancient Egypt'.

The style of writing of an encyclopedia entry is very much more explanatory than that of a dictionary. It is factual rather than linguistic. Rather than defining a word and giving its sources, technical details about a subject or topic are given.

Extracts on pages 351 and 352 from *Compact Encyclopedia* (Geddes & Grosset, 2008)

drainage   GEOGRAPHY AND GEOLOGY   **earthquake**

tions permit, e.g. if the water table is near to the surface, creating a spring, or the geology is such that an artesian well (*see* AQUIFER) is created, then an oasis may develop within a hot desert, providing an island of green.

Hot deserts are found in Africa, Australia, the United States, Chile and cold deserts in the Arctic, eastern Argentina and mountainous regions. Some hot desert extremes are:

extreme of shade temperature: Death Valley, California maximum 28°C (82°F); maximum daily range 41°C (106°F)

max. ground surface temperature: Sahara 78°C (172°F)

extreme of rainfall: Chicama, Peru, 4mm (0.15in) per year

The process whereby desert conditions and processes extend to new areas adjacent to existing deserts is called *desertification*.

drainage the movement of water derived from rain, snowfall and the melting of ice and snow on land (and through it in subterranean waterways) that results eventually in its discharge into the sea. Underlying rocks, how they are arranged and whether there are any structural features that the water may follow influence the flow of streams and rivers. Further factors affecting drainage include soil type, climate and the influence of people.

There are a number of recognisable patterns that can be related to the geology:

dendritic	a random branching unaffected
trellis	by surface rocks; streams aligned with the trend of underlying rocks.
parallel	streams running parallel to each other because of folded rocks or steep slopes with little vegetation.
rectangular	controlled by faults and joints, the latter often in igneous rocks.
annular	formation of streams in circular patterns around a structure of the same shape (e.g. an igneous intrusion).
barbed	a drainage pattern where the tributaries imply a direction of flow contrary to what actually happens.
radial	streams flowing outwards from a higher area.

centripetal	the flow of streams into a central depression where there may be a lake or river.

When a drainage pattern is a direct result of the underlying geology, it is said to be *accordant* (the opposite case being *discordant*).

earthquake movement of the earth, which is often violent, caused by the sudden release of stress that may have accumulated over a long period. Waves of disturbance—*seismic* waves—spread out from the origin, or *focus*, of the earthquake, which is most likely to be movement along a FAULT, although some are associated with volcanic activity.

Earthquakes are classified by their depth of focus: shallow (less than 70 kilometres/44 miles); intermediate (70–300 kilometres/44–187 miles); deep (more than 300 kilometres/187 miles).

Over three-quarters of earthquake energy is concentrated in a belt around the Pacific. This is because most seismic activity occurs at the margins of tectonic plates (*see* PLATE TECTONICS). This means that certain regions of the world are more likely to suffer earthquakes, e.g. the West Coast of North and South America, Japan, the Philippines, Southeast Asia and New Zealand.

Areas of earthquake activity

The effects of earthquakes are naturally very alarming and can be quite catastrophic. Near the focus, ground waves actually throw the land surface about. Surface effects may include the opening of fissures (large cracks), the breaking of roads and pipes, buckling and twisting of railroad lines, and the collapse of bridges and buildings. Secondary effects can be equally destructive if the ground vibrations initiate landslides, avalanches and TSUNAMI

23

chrysalis **classification**

males and females. The 23rd pair are the sex chromosomes, which in males look like an XY and in females an XX. Although the chromosomes look similar in all individuals belonging to a particular species, the genes that they carry are all slightly different, hence each one is totally unique. *See also* HEREDITY and MUTATION.

chrysalis *see* LARVA AND METAMORPHOSIS.

circuit an electrically conducting path that when complete allows a current to flow through it. A circuit may be very simple consisting merely of a battery connected by copper wire to a bulb and then back to the opposite terminal of the battery. When cells and batteries were first made (in the early 1800s by the Italian scientist, Count Alessandro Volta), how charge moved around a circuit remained a mystery. The convention became that current flowed as a positive charge from the positive terminal around to the negative terminal. This is contrary to what actually happens since electrons flow in the opposite direction, but the convention remains (*see also* ELECTRICITY).

A simple circuit diagram

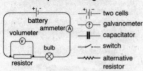

circulation (of the blood) the process by which blood is moved around an animal's body by the pumping action of the heart. The blood carries oxygen and food to all the cells of the body and also takes carbon dioxide from them to the lungs where it is eliminated. Blood that contains oxygen (*oxygenated blood*) is pumped through blood vessels called *arteries* by the left side of the heart. As the arteries reach the tissues and organs they become very tiny (*arterioles* and *capillaries*). Here blood releases its oxygen (becoming *deoxygenated*), and this is picked up and used by cells. Cells release carbon dioxide into the deoxygenated blood as it passes through more capillaries. The blood is now transported through tiny vessels (*venules*) that

become larger *veins* and then it passes back to the right side of the heart. From here it passes to the lungs where carbon dioxide is released and oxygen is picked up before it returns to the left side of the heart once again.

This type of blood circulation is described as 'double'. The heart is divided into two sides, each acting as an independent pump with no communication between them. Each side is further divided into two chambers, the upper one is called the *atrium* and collects incoming blood, passing it to the lower *ventricle*. This is a strong, muscular pump that contracts and pumps blood out either to the body or to the lungs. Arteries always carry oxygenated blood, except for the pulmonary artery which takes blood from the heart to the lungs. Veins always transport deoxygenated blood, except for the pulmonary vein which takes oxygenated blood from the lungs to the heart.

Systemic and pulmonary circulation

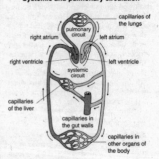

class *see* CLASSIFICATION.

classification a means of grouping living organisms together according to how similar they are to each other. For the early biologists, the physical similarities between organisms were the most important feature, but increasingly in modern times the similarities between organisms at a genetic level have become more important in understanding their relationships.

One main method of classification is most commonly recognised, and this was

Reference works

Atlas

An atlas is a collection of maps. Traditionally, these maps were bound in a book, but they are now also available in digital formats. Maps are usually organised alphabetically under geographical, political and historical categories. The best way to find the map you are looking for is by searching in the table of contents or in the index, as in the following extracts:

Contents

Extracts on pages 353 and 354 from *Atlas of the World* (Geddes & Grosset, 2008)

Map Index

Reference works

Directory

A directory is a list of individuals and organisations that is organised alphabetically or thematically with details such as names, addresses, telephone numbers or other data.

Examples of this sort of reference material are a telephone directory, the 'Who's Who' directory of people who are 'influential' and 'noteworthy' and directories of major towns, cities and countries in the world. Directories are very useful if you are looking for information about a particular person or place. If you are an investigative journalist, you will be used to thumbing through hard copy or digital directories!

Reference for writers

There are many reference works out there which are specifically geared towards writers, or are particularly useful for those writing creatively – either fiction or non-fiction. Among these are:

Writers' and Artists' Yearbook

Published annually, this is an up-to-date guide to getting published, filled with advice and information for writers.

http://www.writersandartists.co.uk/

Rhyming dictionary

There are many different rhyming dictionaries out there. These are of obvious use to poets and song-writers, but are a helpful tool for lots of other types of writer, too. For example, those writing headlines or titles for articles may find inspiration here.

Grammar books

There are many different grammar and usage books available, for all different needs – whether you are a grammar fiend or the word 'grammar' alone is enough to send you running for cover. They range from the dry and factual to the informal and chatty, even funny! Be sure to read blurbs and reviews before buying to get an idea of level, content and tone.

Emotional thesaurus

This is a more unusual one, but is a fantastic idea for fiction writers. The thesaurus lists many different emotions alongside the physical cues, internal sensations and mental responses which are associated with experiencing that emotion – ideal for writers who wish to make their character's behaviour and mentality as realistic as possible. There are also lists of potential future results associated with each emotion, which can help with plot development ideas. Try *The Emotional Thesaurus: A Writer's Guide to Character Expression* by Angela Ackerman and Becca P Puglisi (2012).

Names books

General baby-name books and sites, and those geared specifically to writers (such as *The Writer's Digest Character Naming Sourcebook* by Sherrilyn Kenyon [Writer's Digest Books, 2010]) can help fiction writers who want to find the ideal name to fit a character.

Inspirational books

The Pocket Muse: Ideas and Inspiration for Writing by Monica Wood (Writer's Digest Books, 2004) and similar books provide prompts and photos to spark ideas and get your creative juices flowing, as well as advice to help all writers.

Quotations books

There are many collections of quotations available, including *The Oxford Dictionary of Quotations*. Reading these provides not only an an excellent opportunity to study the power of a carefully considered, well-structured sentence. It is also an opportunity to consider themes, to spark ideas and to draw inspiration.

WRITING YOUR OWN NON-FICTION COMPOSITION

We have looked at a number of different types of fiction writing, and what they involve. We're now going to look at the things you need to keep in mind when you are writing your own non-fiction composition – whether that is a biography, a cookery book, a travel article or a computer manual.

Research

Research is essential in non-fiction. You need to know your subject or topic thoroughly before you write about it, and that means that you need good research skills. Here are some points to help you.

What information are you looking for?
Think back to Chapter 3 and the advice given on

writing for learning. It sounds obvious, but it's worth saying again: you need to know what you're looking for before you start looking for it. What is your subject or topic? Who is the person you are writing a biography about? Which phone are you writing a manual for? Which aspects does your travel article have to cover? Once you know this, you can start looking for appropriate research material.

Where can you find that information?

There are many different types and source of information, but the main ones for non-fiction writing are:

- **primary sources** – such as people, interview transcripts, diaries, letters, original artefacts, data and photographs
- **secondary sources** – such as the reference materials listed above, books, journals and the internet

Looking for information can be daunting, so use all the help you can get.

When you are researching and using **primary sources,** make sure you do the following:

Writing your own non-fiction composition

- Check that they are authentic.
- Ensure that you have permission to use them – is Mrs Brown happy for you to use her grandmother's shortbread recipe in your charity cookery book?
- Check that you have all the information you need from your interview before you leave – you probably won't be able to go back and ask further questions.

When you are looking for **secondary sources** try the following:

- Look through the contents page and index of reference material – this will tell you quickly whether the information you are looking for is there.
- Ask the librarian for help if you are having problems using the library cataloguing system.
- Stay focussed! Don't go wandering off onto websites that have nothing to do with your project.
- Stick to two or three sources on the internet at one time. You can come back for more.
- Don't go past the first page of your search engine.

- Don't believe everything you read on the internet – stick to reputable sites. If in doubt, ask around.

And remember, you can't beat first-hand experience as a form of research. If you are writing about a place to spend the night, then you won't get the information you need from the internet – you have to go there yourself and check it out.

Accuracy

Accuracy is also essential in non-fiction writing. You can let your imagination run riot when you are writing fiction, but you must get your facts straight if you are writing a recipe or telling somebody how to assemble a television stand. Your reader won't be very happy if they burn their food because you told them it was 60 minutes at 120 degrees, rather than 120 minutes at 60 degrees!

And if there is a health and safety aspect to what you are writing, you must be particularly careful about accuracy because people's safety could be put at risk.

For example, if you have to prepare an instruction leaflet about how to set up and connect a television or DVD and your instructions

Writing your own non-fiction composition

are wrong, you could potentially cause a very dangerous situation.

If in doubt, ask somebody else to check what you've written and actually try it out.

Organising your information

Now that you have researched your information, don't let it overwhelm you. Organise it and you'll be able to use it effectively:

- Keep going back to your subject or topic. What information are you looking for?
- Plan your writing, so you know what your structure is going to be.
- Ignore any information that is too detailed or not relevant.
- Remember to write down the author, title, place of publication, publisher, date of publication, page numbers and web addresses for articles from books, journals, periodicals, encyclopedias. Make sure that web links are current at the time of writing, and convert them to working hyperlinks. This way, you will build a bibliography as you go along.

Acknowledging sources/copyright

This last point is very important. You must identify all the material in your biography, article, manual, instruction leaflet or scientific paper that is not your own – no matter where it comes from or what it is. If you copy text, diagrams, photographs, art, music or web pages without acknowledging their source, then you are infringing copyright law, and could be prosecuted.

Copyright stays with the originator during his or her lifetime, and with the heirs to their estate for 70 years after their death.

References

Because of the copyright issue, you should make a list of all the references to books, journals, periodicals and websites you have used in your work. You should also acknowledge primary sources that you have used, and actually make sure that you are allowed to use them.

Refer back to Chapter 3 for more detailed information about how to present references. This will only really apply if you are doing a piece of traditional technical writing.

Beware cut and paste and plagiarism!

Copying and pasting text into your own work without using quotation marks or citing it appropriately is a form of plagiarism.

Plagiarism is when you take somebody else's ideas or writing and present them as your own. If you do this, you will probably fail your essay or thesis.

When you are taking notes, decide what information you need from your source, and then write or summarise it in your own words. That way, you won't be tempted – consciously or subconsciously – to copy the source, word for word.

Don't cut and paste from the internet. You can easily forget that you have taken somebody else's work and put it into your own – especially if you change the font to the one you are using.

Remember that plagiarism is cheating.

Style and tone

The style and tone of your writing will very much depend on what it is and what its purpose is. For example, a travel article will be informal and chatty, while a scientific paper will be objective and factual.

Planning your composition

Once you have researched and gathered your information for your non-fiction composition, you will need to plan it.

Here are some tips to help you do this:

- Get a piece of paper and write down all your ideas. Don't worry about perfect writing at this point – just get the content down.

- Get a clean piece of paper. Put the topic box in the middle of the page.

- Now think about your main ideas – what are they?

- Draw lines from the topic box to these main ideas.

- Now add information where you think it sits within these main ideas.

- Make links between the main ideas.

Structuring your composition

Once you've got your plan worked out, it's time to structure your composition. Again, this will vary according to what you are writing. Have a look at the suggestions on the next two pages.

Writing your own non-fiction composition

Biography

The structure of a biography might look like this:

- Contents
- Prologue
- The early years and influences
- The middle years
- The later years
- Bibliography
- List of illustrations
- Index

Recipe collection

The structure of a recipe collection or cookery book might look like this:

- Foreword
- Acknowledgements
- Introduction
- Starters
- Main courses
- Salads and vegetables
- Desserts
- Equipment
- Index

Staying relevant, objective and factual

Operating instructions for a communication camera

The structure for operating instructions might look like this:

- Safety precautions
- Handling precautions
- Installation
- Connection
- Using the camera
- Maintenance
- Specifications
- Warranty

Staying relevant, objective and factual

Structuring your non-fiction composition will help you to stay relevant, objective and factual.

If you wander off subject, your reader will lose interest and give up cooking the recipe, looking for a decent restaurant to eat in or putting the chest of drawers together. And just because you don't like the owner of the hotel or restaurant doesn't mean to say that he provides bad food or service.

We've already covered the need for accuracy and facts – but it's worth saying again that you need to get your facts right!

Writing your own non-fiction composition

The writing process – non-fiction

Like all types of writing, there is a process for writing non-fiction. Aspects of this process will vary slightly, depending on the genre, or type of non-fiction you are writing. But it will help you to focus your thoughts and give you somewhere to start on your biography, manual, recipe book, travel article, scientific paper – or whatever!

Here's the suggested process:

- **Define the purpose of this piece of writing.** Why are you writing it and who are your readers? If you are writing a short biography, who is it about and who wants to know about them? If you are writing a manual, who will be using it? If you are writing an engineering paper, who and what is it for?
- **Research the information you need.** This will obviously depend on what you are writing. You might need to interview people, use the internet or look in an archive or museum to get the information you need. If you are compiling a recipe book, you will probably have to get into the kitchen and try some of the recipes out yourself.

The writing process – non-fiction

- **Plan and structure.** Again, this will depend on what you are writing. The structure of a biography will be based on the sequence of events in a person's life. A recipe book will probably be divided into categories like starters, main courses and desserts. An instruction leaflet to set up a DVD will go through a strict sequential process from opening up the box to pressing the 'on' button. Whatever the subject or topic, a clear plan and structure will help you to make sense of all the information you have gathered, and this will help you to produce an organised, clear and concise piece of writing.

- **Write your first draft.** Do a rough draft – don't worry too much about how it looks at this stage – just get the information down on paper.

- **Revise and edit.** Refer back to Chapter 2 for advice.

- **Identify any missing information.** Revising and editing your writing usually reveals any gaps that need to be filled.

- **Cut out what you don't need.** The editing process also reveals what you don't need!

- **Write the final draft.** Give it to a 'critical friend' to look over.

KEEP READING AND WRITING

KEEP READING

The quickest way to better English writing is to keep reading – anything and everything you can get your hands on!

Here's a list to get you started.

Newspapers

There are newspapers published in English in every country in the world – many of them online. They will keep you up-to-date with current affairs as well as improving your English. Look out for the 'five Ws and an H' structure and keep an eye out for spin! The more you read, the more you will be able to analyse how writing skills and techniques are being used.

Magazines and ezines

As with newspapers, there are magazines published in English all over the world, and there is now a huge selection of ezines on the internet. They cover all different sorts of interests and topics so read up on your favourite hobby while you are improving your English language skills.

Fiction

There are some wonderful books out there. It can be overwhelming thinking about where to start. Think about reading some of the classics, like *Jane Eyre* by Charlotte Brontë, *To Kill a Mockingbird* by Harper Lee, *Oliver Twist* by Charles Dickens and *Pride and Prejudice* by Jane Austen. If a book has won a prize like the Man Booker Prize or the Pulitzer Prize it is usually (though not always) an indication that the book is going to be worth reading and is likely to reveal exemplary writing skills.

Choose from the great writers of the different genres of fiction: John Buchan (thrillers), Ray Bradbury (science fiction), Robert Louis Stevenson (adventure), Raymond Chandler (crime), Bram Stoker (horror), Emily Brontë (romance). Often genres are more useful for booksellers than readers but it's a starting point.

Look for writers who challenge our conception

of the role of narrator such as Italo Calvino and Vladimir Nabokov. And writers who pay particular attention to the inner lives of their characters such as Iris Murdoch, Fyodor Dostoyevsky, Leo Tolstoy, George Eliot and Marcel Proust.

Look at writers who defy categorisation such as Muriel Spark. Spark's minimalist narratives, especially in her later work, leave as many things unstated as stated. Other writers who have a somewhat similar approach to narrative are Evelyn Waugh and Ivy Compton Burnett.

Read writers in translation such as Calvino, Dostoyevsky, Tolstoy, Proust, Emile Zola, Gabriel Garcia Marquez and Haruki Murakami. Consider the great responsibility that a translator has in interpreting these works.

Non-fiction

Read the biographies and autobiographies of your favourite actors, politicians, sportsmen or women or musicians. Read travel journals and histories. Read recipe books (some people do that for pure enjoyment). Assess how well manuals and instruction leaflets are doing their job.

Keep reading

Textbooks and 'how to' materials

If you enjoyed using this book, there are also lots of other textbooks and 'how to' books available that will help you with spelling, grammar, punctuation, vocabulary and general writing skills.

Blogs

Go online and read some interesting blogs. There are an overwhelming number of them out there so why not start by looking for those on subjects in which you are interested. Some blogs are better than others, but again, you can use your own knowledge and skills to analyse them. Note which blogs you enjoy reading, and why. Ask yourself what it is about the writer's style and approach that you like.

Newsletters

Again, there are lots of newsletters out there, and if you go into any business website, you will probably find they are using an online newsletter as a marketing tool.

If you buy a product online, you will probably receive a newsletter regularly from the company to tell you about new products and offers.

Clubs and groups often produce newsletters to tell members about forthcoming events and exciting news. Look at these with a critical eye. Have they been well written? Do they communicate information clearly and concisely? Are they appropriate for the audience? If not, how would you improve them?

KEEP WRITING

Practice makes perfect – so write whenever you have the opportunity. Here are some suggestions to get you writing regularly:

Diary
Keep a diary. Record your thoughts, feelings and the events of the day every day, or as often as you can. You never know, it could become an important archive one day! Think of Anne Frank, Samuel Pepys, the *Journals* of Captain Cook and Charles Darwin's *Beagle* diary.

Blog
You could start up a blog and air your thoughts about

issues or ideas you are interested in. Or you could start a blog about a hobby or interest that you are enthusiastic about and want to share with others.

Letters and cards
Write letters to friends and family telling them your news. Or send a card to say thank you for a present or for an invitation to dinner. People love to receive letters and cards in the post – it's more personal than an email.

Essays and compositions
If you are a student, the more essays and compositions you write, the more your writing skills will develop and the better your writing will be.

Newspapers
Try writing articles and features for your local newspaper and send them to the editor. You never know – you might get them published. Write about something that you feel strongly about, or that you know a lot about.

Magazines and ezines
You could also try writing articles on your

particular interest or hobby and sending them to magazine and ezine editors. The number of ezines in particular is growing every week, so you could find one that you could contribute to on a regular basis. Or you could set up your own!

Good luck and keep writing!

Now that you have finished this book, you will have (hopefully!) learned plenty of tips and techniques to improve your written English and make it more readable and interesting. You will be able to write clearly and effectively, and to come across in a memorable and professional way.

Good luck and keep writing!

REFERENCES

Better writing for every day

Plain English Campaign
www.plainenglish.co.uk
The Plain English Campaign website is an excellent resource for tips and techniques on how to write clearly and concisely. This description of their work is taken from the website:

> Since 1979, we have been campaigning against gobbledygook, jargon and misleading public information. We have helped many government departments and other official organisations with their documents, reports and publications. We believe that everyone should have access to clear and concise information.
>
> The campaign officially began after founder Chrissie Maher OBE publicly shredded hundreds of official documents in Parliament Square, London. Entirely independent, the campaign funds itself through its commercial services, which include editing and training. We have worked with thousands of organisations ranging from UK Government

Keep writing

departments to World Bowls, helping them make sure their public information is as clear as possible.

We have over 12,000 members in 80 countries and our Crystal Mark is now firmly established as a guarantee that a document is written in plain English. It appears on more than 21,000 documents.

Writing for learning

English–Welsh Phrasebook by D Islwyn Edwards (Waverley Books, 2012)

National Qualifications Curriculum Support: The origins and development of the Cold War, 1945–85 (Learning and Teaching Scotland, 2008)
Available from: Education Scotland
http://www.educationscotland.gov.uk/resources/nq/h/nqresource_tcm4504762.asp

Writing for work or business
Line drawings by Mark Mechan.

Front Door Apartments
http://www.frontdoorapartments.co.uk/

Writing for the media
Style guide courtesy of Waverley Books.

Cake Masters
http://www.cakemasters.co.uk/
http://issuu.com/cakemasters

Shutterstock/zig8 (people playing flute and violin)
Shutterstock/Tatiana Popova (sheet music image)

Mad About Macarons
http://madaboutmacarons.com/

Sue Reid Sexton
http://suereidsexton.blogspot.co.uk/

www.tomorrow.is
Directing editor: Tristan Stewart-Robertson; design:
Tim Fraser Brown; web development: David Gracie.

Writing creatively
Fiction
The Open Window by Saki (H H Munro). Available
to download from:
www.gutenberg.org/ebooks/269

Pride and Prejudice by Jane Austen. Available to download from:
www.gutenberg.org/ebooks/1342

Non-fiction
James Joyce by David Pritchard (Geddes & Grosset, 2001).

Robert Burns in Your Pocket (Waverley Books, 2009).

History, heritage & haute cuisine by Garry Fraser (The Scots Magazine, Nov. 2012, pp. 15–19). Copyright © DC Thomson & Co Ltd.

We fell in love with Zebedee by Andrew Cawley (*The Sunday Post* Travel and Homes, 13 Jan. 2013, pp. 10–11). Copyright © DC Thomson & Co Ltd.

Travels with a Donkey in the Cévennes by Robert Louis Stevenson. Available to download from:
www.gutenberg.org/ebooks/535

Venice and the Veneto (Lonely Planet City Guides) by Alison Bing (Lonely Planet Publications, 2012). Copyright © Lonely Planet.

Writing creatively

Mad about Macarons by Jill Colonna (Waverley Books, 2010). Copyright © Jill Colonna.

The Beginner's Guide to Computers by David McCormick (Geddes & Grosset, 2005)

NetLogo user guide: Wilensky, U (1999) http://ccl. northwestern.edu/netlogo/. Center for Connected Learning and Computer-Based Modeling, North-western University, Evanston, IL.

Yoga and Meditation by Katherine Wright (Geddes & Grosset, 2007).

Introduction to Molecular Motion in Polymers by Richard A. Pethrick, Taweechai Amornsakchai and Alastair M. North (Whittles Publishing, 2011). Copyright © Whittles Publishing.

Surviving Teenagers by Dr David Fong (Geddes & Grosset, 2007)

Quit Smoking by Dr David Fong (Geddes & Grosset, 2007)

Keep writing

It's Not Rocket Science: Learn to Swim (Waverley Books, 2012)

Word Power English Dictionary, Betty Kirkpatrick (Geddes & Grosset, 2013)

Student Dictionary & Thesaurus (Geddes & Grosset, for Reader's Digest, 2007)

Scottish Place Names by George Mackay (Geddes & Grosset, 2003)

Word Power English Thesaurus, Betty Kirkpatrick (Geddes & Grosset, 2013)

Compact Encyclopedia (Geddes & Grosset, 2008)

World Atlas (Geddes & Grosset, 2008)